Sexual Issues

Sexual Issues

Resources for Strategic Pastoral Counseling

Harold Wahking
and Gene Zimmerman

 Baker Books

A Division of Baker Book House Co
Grand Rapids, Michigan 49516

© 1994 by Harold Wahking and Gene Zimmerman

Published by Baker Books
a division of Baker Book House Company
P.O. Box 6287, Grand Rapids, MI 49516-6287

Printed in the United States of America

Library of Congress Cataloging-in-Publication Data

Wahking, Harold L.
    Sexual issues : resources for strategic pastoral counseling / Harold Wahking and Gene Zimmerman.
       p.   cm. — (Resources for strategic pastoral counseling)
    Includes bibliographical references (p.   ).
    ISBN 0-8010-9728-2
    1. Pastoral counseling. 2. Sex counseling. 3. Sex—Religious aspects—Christianity. I. Zimmerman, Gene. II. Title. III. Series.
    BV4012.2.W34   1994
    253.5—dc20   94-5939

In gratitude for all those Christian mentors and friends who taught and shared with me that God's love and grace means joy and fulfillment in every aspect of our human life.

Gene Zimmerman

Thirty-three years ago my Clinical Pastoral Education supervisor, Clarence Barton, and my major seminary professor, Samuel Southard, called me into their office and asked me, "Harold, how would you like to be chaplain of a state mental hospital?" That is how God called me to a specialized ministry in Christian counseling. This book is dedicated to them as an expression of my appreciation for their teaching and modeling.

Harold Wahking

Contents

An Introduction to Strategic Pastoral Counseling

David G. Benner

While the provision of spiritual counsel has been an integral part of Christian soul care since the earliest days of the church, the contemporary understanding and practice of pastoral counseling is largely a product of the twentieth century. Developing within the shadow of the modern psychotherapies, pastoral counseling has derived much of its style and approach from these clinical therapeutics. What this has meant is that pastoral counselors have often seen themselves more as counselors than as pastors and the counseling that they have provided has often been a rather awkward adaptation of clinical counseling models to a pastoral context. This, in turn, has often resulted in significant tension between the pastoral and psychological dimensions of the counseling provided by clergy and others in Christian ministry. It is also frequently reflected in pastoral counselors who are more interested in anything connected with the modern mystery cult of psychotherapy than with their own tradition of Christian soul care, and who, as a consequence, are often quite insecure in their pastoral role and identity.

While pastoral counseling owes much to the psychological culture that has gained ascendancy in the West during the past century, this influence has quite clearly been a mixed blessing. Contemporary pastoral counselors typically offer their help with much more psychological sophistication than was the case several decades ago, but all too often they do so without a clear sense of the uniqueness of counseling that is offered by a pastor. And not only are the distinctive spiritual resources of Christian ministry often deemphasized or ignored, but the tensions that are associated with attempts to directly translate clinical models of counseling into the pastoral context become a source of much frustration. This is in part why so many pastors report dissatisfaction with their counseling. While they indicate that this dissatisfaction is a result of insufficient training in and time for counseling, a bigger part of the problem may be that pastors have been offered approaches to counseling that are of questionable appropriateness for the pastoral context and that will inevitably leave them feeling frustrated and inadequate.

Strategic Pastoral Counseling is a model of counseling that has been specifically designed to fit the role, resources, and needs of the typical pastor who counsels. Information about this "typical" pastor was solicited by means of a survey of over 400 pastors (this research is described in the introductory volume of the series, *Strategic Pastoral Counseling: A Short-Term Structured Model* [Benner 1992]). The model appropriates the insights of contemporary counseling theory without sacrificing the resources of pastoral ministry. Furthermore, it takes its form and direction from the pastoral role and in so doing offers an approach to counseling that is not only congruent with the other aspects of pastoral ministry but that places pastoral counseling at the very heart of ministry.

The present volume represents an application of Strategic Pastoral Counseling to one commonly encountered problem situation. As such, it presupposes a familiarity with the basic model. Readers not familiar with *Strategic Pastoral Counseling: A Short-Term Structured Model* should consult this book for a detailed presentation of the model and its implementation. What follows is a brief review of this material which, while it does not adequately summarize all that is presented in that book, should serve as a reminder of the most important features of the Strategic Pastoral Counseling approach.

The Strategic Pastoral Counseling Model

Strategic Pastoral Counseling is short-term, bibliotherapeutic, wholistic, structured, spiritually focused, and explicitly Christian. Each of these characteristics will be briefly discussed in order.

Short-Term Counseling

Counseling can be brief (that is, conducted over a relatively few sessions), time-limited (that is, conducted within an initially fixed number of total sessions), or both. Strategic Pastoral Counseling is both brief and time-limited, working within a suggested maximum of five sessions. The decision to set this upper limit on the number of sessions was in response to the fact that the background research conducted in the design of the model indicated that 87 percent of the pastoral counseling conducted by pastors in general ministry involves five sessions or less. This short-term approach to counseling seems ideally suited to the time availability, training, and role demands of pastors.

Recent research in short-term counseling has made it clear that while such an approach requires that the counselor be diligent in maintaining the focus on the single agreed upon central problem, significant and enduring changes can occur through a very small number of counseling sessions. Strategic Pastoral Counseling differs, in this regard, from the more ongoing relationship of discipleship or spiritual guidance. In these, the goal is the development of spiritual maturity. Strategic Pastoral Counseling has a much more modest goal: examining a particular problem or experience in the light of God's will for and activity in the life of the individual seeking help and attempting to facilitate growth in and through that person's present life situation. While this is still an ambitious goal, its focused nature makes it quite attainable within a short period of time. It is this focus that makes the counseling strategic.

The five-session limit should be communicated by the pastor no later than the first session and preferably in the prior conversation when the time is set for this session. This ensures that the parishioner is aware of the time limit from the beginning and can share responsibility in keeping the counseling sessions focused. Some people will undoubtedly require more than five sessions in order to bring about a resolution of their problems. These people should be referred to someone who is appropriately qualified for such work; preparation for this referral will be one of the goals of the five sessions. However, the fact that such people may require more help than can be provided in five sessions of pastoral counseling does not mean that they cannot benefit from such focused short-term pastoral care; no individuals should be regarded as inappropriate candidates for Strategic Pastoral Counseling merely because they may require other help.

One final but important note about the suggested limit of five sessions is that this does not have to be tied to a corresponding period of five weeks. In fact, many pastors find weekly sessions to be less useful than sessions scheduled two or three weeks apart. This sort of spacing of the last couple sessions is particularly helpful and should be considered even if the first several sessions are held weekly.

Bibliotherapeutic Counseling

Bibliotherapy refers to the therapeutic use of reading. Strategic Pastoral Counseling builds the use of written materials into the heart of its approach to pastoral caregiving. The Bible itself is, of course, a rich bibliotherapeutic resource and the encouragement of and direction in its reading is an important part of Strategic Pastoral Counseling. Its use must be disciplined and selective and particular care must be taken to ensure that it is never employed in a mechanical or impersonal manner. However, when used appropriately it can unquestionably be one of the most dynamic and powerful resources available to the pastor who counsels.

While the Bible is a unique bibliotherapeutic resource, it is not the only such resource. Strategic Pastoral Counseling comes with a built-in set of specifically designed resources. Each of the 10 volumes in this series has an accompanying book written for the parishioner who is being seen in counseling. These resource books are written by the same authors as the volumes for pastors and are designed for easy integration into counseling sessions.

The use of reading materials that are consistent with the counseling being provided can serve as a most significant support and extension of the counseling offered by a pastor. The parishioner now has a helping resource that is not limited by the pastor's time and availability. Furthermore, the pastor can now allow the written materials to do part of the work of counseling, using the sessions to deal with those matters that are not as well addressed through the written page.

Wholistic Counseling

It might seem surprising to suggest that a short-term counseling approach should also be wholistic. But this is both possible and highly desirable. Wholistic counseling is counseling that is responsive to the totality of the complex psycho-spiritual dynamics that make up the life of human persons. Biblical psychology is clearly a wholistic psychology. The various "parts" of persons (i.e., body, soul, spirit, heart, flesh, etc.) are never presented as separate faculties or independent components of persons but always as different ways of seeing the whole person. Biblical discussions of persons emphasize first and foremost their essential unity of being. Humans are ultimately understandable only in the light of this primary and irreducible wholeness and helping efforts that are truly Christian must resist the temptation to see persons only through their thoughts, feelings, behaviors, or any other single manifestation of being.

The alternative to wholism in counseling is to focus on only one of these modalities of functioning and this is, indeed, what many approaches to counseling do. In contrast, Strategic Pastoral Counseling asserts that pastoral counseling must be responsive to the behavioral (action), cognitive (thought), and affective (feeling) elements of personal functioning. Each examined separately can obscure that which is really going on with a person. But taken together they form the basis for a comprehensive assessment and effective intervention. Strategic Pastoral Counseling provides a framework for ensuring that each of these spheres of functioning is addressed and this, in fact, provides much of the structure for the counseling.

Structured Counseling

The structured nature of Strategic Pastoral Counseling is that which enables its brevity, ensuring that each of the sessions has a clear focus and that each builds upon the previous ones in contributing toward the accomplishment of the overall goals. The framework that structures Strategic Pastoral Counseling is sufficiently tight as to enable the pastor to provide a wholistic assessment and counseling intervention within a maximum of five sessions and yet it is also sufficiently flexible to allow for differences in individual styles of different counselors. This is very important because Strategic Pastoral Counseling is not primarily a set of techniques but an intimate encounter of and dialogue between people.

The structure of Strategic Pastoral Counseling grows out of the goal of addressing the feelings, thoughts, and behaviors that are part of the troubling experiences of the person seeking help. It is also a structure that is responsive to the several tasks that face the pastoral counselor, tasks such as conducting an initial assessment, developing a general understanding of the problem and of the person's major needs, and selecting and delivering interventions and resources that will bring help. This structure is described in more detail later.

Spiritually Focused Counseling

The fourth distinctive of Strategic Pastoral Counseling is that it is spiritually focused. This does not mean that only religious matters are discussed. Our spirituality is our essential heart commitments, our basic life direction, and our fundamental allegiances. These spiritual aspects of our being are, of course, reflected in our attitudes toward God and are expressed in our explicitly religious values and behaviors. However, they are also reflected in matters that may seem on the surface to be much less religious. Strategic Pastoral Counselors place a primacy on listening to this underlying spiritual story. They listen for what we might call the story behind the story.

But listening to the story behind the story requires that one first listen to and take seriously the presenting story. To disregard the presenting situation is spiritualization of a problem. It fails to take the problem seriously and makes a mockery of counseling as genuine dialogue. The Strategic Pastoral Counselor thus listens to and enters into the experience of parishioners as they relate their struggles and life's experiences. But while this is a real part of the story, it is not the whole story that must be heard and understood. For in the midst of this story emerges another: the story of their spiritual response to these experiences. This response may be one of unwavering trust in God but a failure to expect much of him. Or it may be one of doubt, anger, confusion, or despair. Each of these is a spiritual response to present struggles and in one form or another, the spiritual aspect of the person's experience will always be discernible to the pastor who watches for it. Strategic Pastoral Counseling makes this underlying spiritual story the primary focus.

Explicitly Christian Counseling

While it is important to not confuse spirituality with religiosity, it is equally important to not confuse Christian spirituality with any of its imitations. In this regard, it is crucial that Strategic Pastoral Counseling be distinctively and explicitly Christian. And while Strategic Pastoral Counseling begins with a focus on spiritual matters understood broadly, its master goal is to facilitate the other person's awareness of and response to the call of God to surrender and service. This is the essential and most important distinctive of Strategic Pastoral Counseling.

One of the ways in which Strategic Pastoral Counseling is made explicitly Christian is through its utilization of Christian theological language, images, and concepts and the religious resources of prayer, Scripture, and the sacraments. These resources must never be used in a mechanical, legalistic, or magical fashion. But used sensitively and wisely, they can be the conduit for a dynamic contact between God and the person seeking pastoral help. And this is the goal of their utilization, not some superficial baptizing of the counseling in order to make it Christian but rather a way of bringing the one seeking help more closely in touch with the God who is the source of all life, growth, and healing.

Another important resource that is appropriated by the Strategic Pastoral Counselor is that of the church as a community. Too often pastoral counseling is conducted in a way that is not appreciably different from that which might be offered by a Christian counselor in private practice. This most unfortunate practice ignores the rich resources that are potentially available in any Christian congregation. One of the most important ways in which Strategic Pastoral Counseling is able to maintain its short-term nature is by the pastor connecting the person seeking help with others in the church who can provide portions of that help. The congregation can, of course, also be involved in less individualistic ways. Support and ministry groups of various sorts are becoming a part of many congregations that seek to provide a dynamic ministry to their community and are potentially important resources for the Strategic Pastoral Counselor.

A final and even more fundamental way in which Strategic Pastoral Counseling is Christian is in the reliance that it encourages on the Holy Spirit. The Spirit is the indispensable source of all wisdom that is necessary for the practice of pastoral counseling. Recognizing that all healing and growth are ultimately of God, the Strategic Pastoral Counselor can thus take comfort in this reliance on the Spirit of God and on the fact that ultimate responsibility for people and their well-being lies with God.

Stages and Tasks of Strategic Pastoral Counseling

The three overall stages that organize Strategic Pastoral Counseling can be described as *encounter, engagement,* and *disengagement.* The first stage of Strategic Pastoral Counseling, encounter, corresponds to the initial session in which the goal is to establish personal contact with the person seeking help, set the boundaries for the counseling relationship, become acquainted with that person and the central concerns, conduct a pastoral diagnosis, and develop a mutually acceptable focus for the subsequent sessions. The second stage, engagement, involves the pastor moving beyond the first contact and establishing a deeper working alliance with the person seeking help. This normally occupies the next one to three sessions and entails the exploration of the person's feelings, thoughts, and behavioral patterns associated with this problem area and the development of new perspectives and strategies for coping or change. The third and final stage, disengagement, describes the focus of the last one or possibly two sessions, and involves an evaluation of progress and an assessment of remaining concerns, the making of a referral for further help if this is needed, and the ending of the counseling relationship. These stages and tasks are summarized in the table below.

Stages and Tasks of Strategic Pastoral Counseling

Stage 1: Encounter (Session 1)
• Joining and boundary-setting
• Exploring the central concerns and relevant history
• Conducting a pastoral diagnosis
• Achieving a mutually agreeable focus for counseling

Stage 2: Engagement (Sessions 2, 3, 4)
• Exploration of cognitive, affective, and behavioral aspects of the problem and the identification of resources for coping or change

Stage 3: Disengagement (Sessions 4, 5)
• Evaluation of progress and assessment of remaining concerns
• Referral (if needed)
• Termination of counseling

The Encounter Stage

The first task in this initial stage of Strategic Pastoral Counseling is joining and boundary-setting. Joining involves putting the parishioner at ease by means of a few moments of casual conversation that is designed to ease pastor and parishioner into contact. Such preliminary conversation should never take more than five minutes and should usually be kept to two or three. It will not always be necessary, because some people are immediately ready to tell their story. Boundary-setting involves the communication of the purpose of this session and the time frame for the session and your work together. This should not normally require more than a sentence or two.

The exploration of central concerns and relevant history usually begins with an invitation for parishioners to describe what led them to seek help at the present time. After hearing an expression of these immediate concerns, it is usually helpful to get a brief historical perspective on these concerns and the person. Ten to fifteen minutes of exploration of the course of development of the presenting problems and their efforts to cope or get help with them is the foundation of this part of the session. It is also important at this point to get some idea of the parishioner's present living and family arrangements as well as work and/or educational situation. The organizing thread for this section of the first interview should be the presenting problem. These matters will not be the only ones discussed but this focus serves to give the session the necessary direction.

Stripped of its distracting medical connotations, diagnosis is problem definition and this is a fundamental part of any approach to counseling. Diagnoses involve judgments about the nature of the problem and, either implicitly or explicitly, pastoral counselors make such judgments every time they commence a counseling relationship. But in order for diagnoses to be relevant they must guide the counseling that will follow. This means that the categories of pastoral assessment must be primarily related to the spiritual focus, which is foundational to any counseling that is appropriately called pastoral. Thus, the diagnosis called for in the first stage of Strategic Pastoral Counseling involves an assessment of the person's spiritual well-being.

The framework for pastoral diagnosis adopted by Strategic Pastoral Counseling is that suggested by Malony (1988) and used as the basis of his Religious Status Interview. Malony proposed that the diagnosis of Christian religious well-being should involve the assessment of the person's awareness of God, acceptance of God's grace, repentance and responsibility, response to God's leadership and direction, involvement in the church, experience of fellowship, ethics, and openness in the faith. While this approach to pastoral diagnosis has been found to be helpful by many, the Strategic Pastoral Counselor need not feel confined by it. It is offered as a suggested framework for conducting a pastoral assessment and each individual pastoral counselor needs to approach this task in ways that fit his or her own theological convictions and personal style. Further details on conducting a pastoral assessment can be found in *Strategic Pastoral Counseling: A Short-Term Structured Model.*

The final task of the encounter stage of Strategic Pastoral Counseling is achieving a mutually agreeable focus for counseling. Often this is self-evident, made immediately clear by the first expression of the parishioner. At other times parishioners will report a wide range of concerns in the first session and will have to be asked what should constitute the primary problem focus. The identification of the primary problem focus leads naturally to a formulation of goals for the counseling. These goals will sometimes be quite specific (i.e., to be able to make an informed decision about a potential job change) but will also at times be rather broad (i.e., to be able to express feelings related to an illness). As is illustrated in these examples, some goals will describe an end-point while others will describe more of a process. Maintaining this flexibility in how goals are understood is crucial if Strategic Pastoral Counseling is to be a helpful counseling approach for the broad range of situations faced by the pastoral counselor.

The Engagement Stage

The second stage of Strategic Pastoral Counseling involves the further engagement of the pastor and the one seeking help around the problems and concerns that brought them together. This is the heart of the counseling process. The major tasks of this stage are the exploration of the person's feelings, thoughts, and behavioral patterns associated with the central concerns and the development of new perspectives and strategies for coping or change.

It is important to note that the work of this stage may well begin in the first session. The model should not be interpreted in a rigid or mechanical manner. If the goals of the first stage are completed with time remaining in the first session, one can very appropriately begin to move into the tasks of this next stage. However, once the tasks of Stage 1 are completed, those associated with this second stage become the central focus. If the full five sessions of Strategic Pastoral Counseling are employed, this second stage normally provides the structure for sessions 2, 3, and 4.

The central foci for the three sessions normally associated with this stage are the feelings, thoughts, and behaviors associated with the problem presented by the person seeking help. Although these are usually intertwined, a selective focus on each, one at a time, ensures that each is adequately addressed and that all the crucial dynamics of the person's psychospiritual functioning are considered.

The reason for beginning with feelings is that this is where most people themselves begin when they come to a counselor. But this does not mean that most people know their feelings. The exploration of feelings involves encouraging people to face and express whatever it is that they are feeling, to the end that these feelings can be known and then dealt with appropriately. The goal at this point is to listen and respond empathically to the feelings of those seeking help, not to try to change them.

After an exploration of the major feelings being experienced by the person seeking help, the next task is an exploration of the thoughts associated with these feelings and the development of alternative ways of understanding present experiences. It is in this phase of Strategic Pastoral Counseling that the explicit use of Scripture is usually most appropriate. Bearing in mind the potential misuses and problems that can be associated with such use of religious resources, the pastoral counselor should be, nonetheless, open to a direct presentation of scriptural truths when they offer the possibility of a new and helpful perspective on one's situation.

The final task of the engagement stage of Strategic Pastoral Counseling grows directly out of this work on understanding and involves the exploration of the behavioral components of the person's functioning. Here the pastor explores what concrete things the person is doing in the face of the problems or distressing situations being encountered and together with the parishioner begins to identify changes in behavior that may be desirable. The goal of this stage is to identify changes that both pastor and parishioner agree are important and to begin to establish concrete strategies for making these changes.

The Disengagement Stage

The last session or two involves preparation for the termination of counseling and includes two specific tasks: the evaluation of progress and assessment of remaining concerns, and making arrangements regarding a referral if this is needed.

The evaluation of progress is usually a process that both pastor and parishioner will find rewarding. Some of this may be done during previous sessions. Even when this is the case, it is a good idea to use the last session to undertake a brief review of what has been learned from the counseling. Closely associated with this, of course, is an identification of remaining concerns. Seldom is everything resolved after five sessions. This means that the parishioner is preparing to leave counseling with some work yet to be done. But he or she does so with plans for the future and the development of these is an important task of the disengagement stage of Strategic Pastoral Counseling.

If significant problems remain at this point, the last couple of sessions should also be used to make referral arrangements. Ideally these should be discussed in the second or third session and they should by now be all arranged. It might even be ideal if by this point the parishioner could have had a first session with the new counselor, thus allowing a processing of this first experience as part of the final pastoral counseling session.

Recognition of one's own limitations of time, experience, training, and ability is an indispensable component of the practice of all professionals. Pastors are no exception. Pastors offering Strategic Pastoral Counseling need, therefore, to be aware of the resources within their community and be prepared to refer parishioners for help that they can better receive elsewhere.

In the vast majority of cases, the actual termination of a Strategic Pastoral Counseling relationship goes very smoothly. Most often both pastor and parishioner agree that there is not further need to meet and they find easy agreement with, even if some sadness around, the decision to discontinue the counseling sessions. However, there may be times when this process is somewhat difficult. This will sometimes be due to the parishioner's desire to continue to meet. At other times the difficulty in terminating will reside within the pastor. Regardless, the best course of action is usually to follow through on the initial limits agreed upon by both parties.

The exception to this rule is a situation where the parishioner is facing some significant stress or crisis at the end of the five sessions and where there are no other available resources to provide the support needed. If this is the situation, an extension of a few sessions may be appropriate. However, this should again be time-limited and should take the form of crisis management. It should not involve more sessions than is absolutely necessary to restore some degree of stability or to introduce the parishioner to other people who can be of assistance.

Conclusion

Strategic Pastoral Counseling provides a framework for pastors who seek to counsel in a way that is congruent with the rest of their pastoral responsibilities and psychologically informed and responsible. While skill in implementing the model comes only over time, because the approach is focused and time-limited it is quite possible for most pastors to acquire these skills. However, counseling skills cannot be adequately learned simply by reading books. As with all interpersonal skills, they must be learned through practice, and ideally, this practice is best acquired in a context of supervisory feedback from a more experienced pastoral counselor.

The pastor who has mastered the skills of Strategic Pastoral Counseling is in a position to proclaim the Word of God in a highly personalized and relevant manner to people who are often desperate for help. This is a unique and richly rewarding opportunity. Rather than scattering seed in a broadcast manner across ground that is often stony and hard even if at places it is also fertile and receptive to growth, the pastoral counselor has the opportunity to carefully plant one seed at a time. Knowing the soil conditions, he or she is also able to plant it in a highly individualized manner, taking pains to ensure that it will not be quickly blown away, and then gently watering and nourishing its growth. This is the unique opportunity for the ministry of Strategic Pastoral Counseling. It is my prayer that pastors will see the centrality of counseling to their call to ministry, feel encouraged by the presence of an approach to pastoral counseling that lies within their skills and time availability, and will take up these responsibilities with renewed vigor and clarity of direction.

Part 1

Foundations
*Counseling People
with Sexual Problems*

1

Strategies for Adding to Your Pastoral Counseling Skills

W ith sermons to prepare, committee meetings to attend, and phone calls to return, we sometimes feel that people who want our counseling help are a burden. At the same time we may also feel that meeting with individuals in private usually helps us apply the truths of the gospel in the very deepest of ways. Most of us end up torn between frustration over not having enough time for counseling and a sense of spiritual excitement in seeing God at work in these one-to-one encounters of healing and hope.

We wish to encourage all pastors who read this book to be thankful to God for the spiritual resources we have from him for helping troubled people. God loves us and forgives us. God calls us to meaningful service as we love one another. God has not given us a spirit of timidity and fear but of love, power, and self-control (2 Tim. 1:7). By living out these and other Christian truths as we meet privately with troubled people, we bring to our counseling powerful and godly helps that many secular therapists do not use.

That you are reading this book is an indication of your interest in people and in working to solve their sexual problems. We believe you have a desire to be helpful in a caring and Christ-like way to people who are having difficulties with their sexuality to such a degree that they are prohibited from celebrating and enjoying this lovely, creative gift of God.

At the outset we would like to state some foundational principles that undergird much of what is shared throughout the pages of this book.

First, God is actively engaged in and through people to restore human life to its fullest and best so that each person may discover and enjoy the many good things that God has given to bless and enrich us. This means that God is actively present with us as we seek help or work to help each other. God is not only present but he acts to bring insight and understanding to the counselor and the counselee for the healing and growth of both. God is always the unseen caring Presence as we seek to understand ourselves, grow in knowledge and truth, and live out in relationships what he has revealed to us.

Second, our gender as male and female is part of the good creation of God and the expressions of our sexuality, both for procreation and for loving pleasure, are part of God's plan and intention (Gen. 1:27, 31).

Third, because human sexuality is such a strong and powerful gift, we must learn to control and express it in ways that will bless and enhance ourselves and others. Many of us have experienced difficulty in understanding and expressing our sexuality. These problems must not obscure the deepest truth about God, God's creation, or our life together. Sexual behavior that enhances authentic love fulfills all God's laws about sex (Gal. 5:14). Maleness that does not demean femaleness but lovingly upholds male traits is godly. Femaleness that does not demean maleness but lovingly upholds female traits is godly. Love, respect, honor, and fidelity make the difference as we deal with sexual issues and other areas of life as well. *Love is the Christian way.*

We love many people of both sexes in ways that do not involve sexual intercourse. The more we can enter into true friendship love, the more prepared we are for entering into the special relationship of Christian marriage and for celebrating that bonded "oneness" through expressions of sexual love. This is God's way to truth and life (John 14:6).

Fourth, we believe that you already have skills and insights that can be brought together and used significantly to help those who are struggling with sexual problems and misunderstandings. You do not have to be a trained therapist to follow the Strategic Pastoral Counseling model. Most of your basic training and personal concern have already prepared you for this ministry. Our intention in this book is to give you additional ways of caring as you make your pastoral help available to others.

Finally, those who counsel others about sexual difficulties must be as fully aware as possible about their own sexuality. Each of us has secrets, fears, and uncertainties. We may find ourselves sexually aroused as we listen to others, repelled by what we hear, or stirred to fantasize as their stories unfold. The awareness of these inner responses allows us to maintain spiritual control and professional perspective. We must recognize our sexual feelings and thoughts but not allow them to control us. This empowers us to make the center of our attention the bringing of God's love to troubled persons.

Suggestions for Making Maximum Use of This Book

Naturally we hope you will read this entire book and mark its pages with your own insights and notes about additional skills for helping people. Part 1, *Foundations*, contains an overview of counseling that may help you with any person you are counseling privately. Part 2, *Applications*, will provide specific help for those times when someone shares a particular sexual problem with you. At that time you may benefit from reviewing the appropriate chapter to establish your pastoral counseling perspective with that individual.

For each specific sexual problem presented, we list books for additional reading. If you are called to become more deeply involved in care for people with some particular sexual need, reading the books mentioned will be both helpful and essential to your special ministry.

In addition, we have provided fictional dialogues between pastors and counselees as they deal with the sexual problems being studied. By comparing what you might have said with the text example, you may grow in awareness of your technique and make changes as you see the need. In the dialogues we have provided a section called "Pastor's Silent Reflections." Our intent is to share with you what the pastor is thinking and feeling as he or she responds to the other person. You may gain much insight into yourself and your own counseling work by comparing these reflections with those you recall from your own work.

You will also notice in the dialogue sections helps called "Commentary." Here we will focus on techniques to use in your counseling work. We will evaluate the pastor's choices in order to assist you in choosing a strategy as you listen to sexually troubled counselees. Use the dialogue sections to help yourself become more perceptive about your hidden emotions and motives; this discernment will empower you to understand people at deeper and deeper levels.

The Person of the Pastor in Counseling

We come to counseling with our own past history, and we cannot turn that off as we listen to counselees. We can, however, manage or cope with that part of our own agenda that comes up in counseling by talking about these feelings with a friend. By doing so we take care of ourselves but not at the counselee's expense.

If a woman hesitantly explains to us that her husband does so little foreplay that she is not vaginally lubricated and thus experiences pain on penile entrance, we may blush, rush in with a suggestion to use K-Y jelly, or quickly urge her to discuss this with her physician. All these responses get in the way of caring effectively for this person in need of love and understanding. Our discomfort gets in the way of helping her initiate changes in her relationship with her husband that will lead to a solution to her physical problem. We need to discuss our feelings with a colleague until we feel confident that we can actually talk with a woman in private about vaginal lubrication without embarrassment!

As children we may have been warned not to talk about sex and cautioned not to ever listen at the bedroom door or otherwise know about the sexuality of our parents or others. Then, as adults, when we need to listen to the intimate sexual details of counselees, we may become anxious. Unconsciously we may feel we are disobeying our parents and will get into trouble.

We may also fear talking about intimate aspects of sex because it is sexually arousing. We may fear that we are feeling lust—and we may be! It is not uncommon to feel sexual stimulation while listening to someone describe sexual problems and needs. Our spiritual task is to acknowledge these feelings within ourselves, all the while remembering that our role in the session is to maintain control of our own feelings so we can care about the other person. Later discussions with colleagues about intense sexual emotions or fantasies may be helpful in understanding both ourselves and the other person.

We may become anxious when we hear about sexual problems because what the other person reveals is related to some of our own sexual concerns. A man tells about how exciting pornography is for him, and we begin recalling similar feelings and actions from our own past. We may then distance ourselves from this person in order to keep from facing our own capacity for sexual arousal in connection with pornography. Our distancing also helps us avoid facing moral chagrin over our own behavior.

There is at least one other way in which the pastor may become emotional in harmful ways while listening to intimate sexual details. We may become sexually excited and then fear that we are voyeurs—and we are to some extent in that situation. It is exciting to delve into the intimate problems of others, especially the first few times we hear about a particular type of difficulty. Fearing our own feelings, we may attempt to shut down the other person by answering, "Jim, just pray about it. God will keep you from going into a porno shop."

The most powerful way to deal with our own emotional needs as we hear people discuss their sexuality is through prayer and consultation with a competent colleague. In prayer we can present ourselves and our feelings, relying on the fact that God knows all about us but loves us anyway. He forgives and restores. Such prayer can be followed by talking with a colleague about the nature of our sexual arousal so that we can understand the illusions and distortions that may be occurring in us. *A special note:* if there is someone we are seeing and having sexual feelings about and if we are strongly resistant to talking with a colleague about that situation, that is the very counseling relationship we most need to discuss. In prayer and confession we can be healed (James 5:16) and empowered to continue to help this person.

Preaching Style and Requests for Counseling

Not only must the pastor be alert to issues of confidentiality and to his or her inner feelings while talking about sexual issues; the pastor must also make prudent and loving decisions about what to say about sexuality in sermons. If we do not mention the topic, many people may unconsciously decide that we are not comfortable talking about that subject. They may then turn elsewhere for help and possibly receive less than Christian care. If, in our sermons, we do include some reference to sexuality or to counseling individuals with sexual problems, what we share will have a vital influence upon whether or not troubled people seek us out.

If we describe a counseling scene, we do well to talk about someone we worked with in a previous pastorate. In most circumstances we may need to ask a person's permission to use the story. Then we need to state to the congregation that we have received permission to share the well disguised story. *We must remove all identifying factors from the stories we tell.* We can change the age of the person and the number of children he or she has. We can tell the story as if it happened last month when it actually occurred years ago. We can change the occupation of the person.

Once we have disguised the story, we must then present the experience with the counselee "winning." In addition, the credit goes to God and the individual, not to the pastor's "great counseling skills."

The illustration we use in the sermon needs to demonstrate how some biblical truth, empowered by the Holy Spirit, helped a hurting person regain healing and hope. Needy people will be turned away if our story shows how the Bible makes people feel guilty and shameful over their sexual errors.

We should make references to sexual problems in the context of other human issues. An entire sermon on sexuality will be threatening to some listeners and perhaps even inappropriate if a number of small children are present. Instead of doing an entire sermon on sexuality we can describe how the Scriptures help us with marital problems, child rearing, depression, alcohol problems, and low self-esteem. In these sermons we can include examples of sexual issues. By showing in sermons how the Bible truly helps people gain new perspective and new joy, we encourage people to seek out our help with their problems.

The Strategic Pastoral Counseling Method with Sexually Troubled People

During the *Encounter* stage (usually a major part of the first few sessions) we work with people to establish a relationship that will sustain intimate conversation about sexual problems. Some people will be very embarrassed. Others will worry that we are embarrassed to hear about their sexual difficulties. Some will fear that we will relate to them as a parent did years ago, perhaps by becoming angry and telling them they are terrible sinners. Many people will unconsciously be asking us whether or not there is any hope for them. Our first task is to tune in not to the sexual problem but to the human being and child of God who has the problem. The quality of our relationship is more important than the information we may bring to bear upon the problem.

In the first or second session we may need to make some statement about confidentiality. A husband may need to pour out some details about an affair in which he is involved and be assured that you will not tell his wife or anyone else.

At this time it is important to set time and session limits as well. You may want to explain about two-thirds of the way through the first session: "I normally see people for about fifty minutes so I will need to stop in about ten more minutes. Also, I usually see people once or twice or up to about five sessions. If their problem is such that more work is required, I normally make a referral to a professional therapist for the remaining sessions needed. My preference is that I see people for the fifth session after they have already had at least one session with the person to whom I have referred them. That way we can all assess the referral and make plans for follow-up. Do you have any questions about the structure of our working together?"

A most important aspect of the *Encounter* phase is to encourage the client to establish a specific focus. If the client exclaims, "I want a happier marriage!" we might respond, "What is one specific change you could make that would lead to more happiness in your marriage?"

One husband complained that his wife did not seem to be very interested in sex. She had gained weight and that turned him off. He thought she needed counseling help.

Pastor: What might you be willing to change about yourself that would help improve your marriage?

Henry: I don't know. *She's* the one with the problem. She says I'm always on her about her weight but I'm just frustrated that she's always too tired or too busy or too sleepy to make love with me.

Pastor: What do you hope to gain by getting on her about her weight?

Henry: That she'll lose weight and look nicer!

Pastor: Is that more important to you than increasing the frequency of your love making?

Henry: Uhhh . . . Well . . . no. I'd rather have more love making.

Pastor: Well, then, are you willing to consider teaching yourself to stop commenting on her weight in order to increase the possibility of more love making?

Henry: I guess so.

Pastor: Well, then, the next time you are inclined to comment on her weight, what might you say to yourself silently?

Henry: I don't know what you mean.

Pastor's Silent Reflections: Poor guy. He's sexually frustrated and angry at his wife. He's probably turning her off by commenting about her weight. He's probably not aware of his motive for making remarks about her weight; he probably sincerely believes he just wants her to lose weight. I'll see.

Pastor: My hunch is that when your wife seems to be uninterested in sexual love with you, you feel angry and disgusted and then perhaps make some comment about her weight. What do you actually do and say?

Henry: Well, now that I think of it, that's what I do some of the time.

Pastor: Thank you for sharing that with me; that's the stuff growth is made of!

Commentary: The pastor does well to thank Henry for opening up; this is a form of encouragement and reinforcement. The pastor also seems to be thinking that when his wife rejects him, Henry unconsciously hurts her in retaliation by commenting on her weight. Henry may become quite anxious if his motives are exposed this early in the first counseling session. The pastor needs to assess the level of trust Henry has for both the pastor and the counseling before moving ahead.

Pastor: What, then, is your motive for commenting on her weight gain?

Henry: I don't know what you mean. I'm just getting angry and telling her about it.

Commentary: Henry may not be ready to face his motives. Or he may not have understood the use of the term "motive" in the question. The pastor might have asked, "What do you hope to gain by commenting on her weight?"

Pastor: Angry over . . . ?

Henry: Her not wanting to have sex with me.

Pastor's Silent Reflections: Henry blocked on facing his hidden motives. Maybe he is ready to take charge of his own feelings about his wife's rejection. I'll explain the principle that emotions are not caused by what other people say and do but by our interpretations of what they say and do. Henry might gain some hope if he sees that he has some control over his feelings.

Pastor: I'd like to make a suggestion now that might help. [Henry agrees to the idea.] Our emotions are not caused by what other people say and do but by our interpretations of what they say and do. By changing our interpretations we can change our feelings. If your wife says "No" the next time you come on to her, you could make the interpretation, "She doesn't love me," and feel rejected. Or, you could make the interpretation, "She doesn't care about my sexual needs," and feel angry. You might interpret her to be saying, "I'm so discouraged about my weight that I am embarrassed to have you see and touch me," and feel sad for her. So the next time she seems uninterested, I wonder if you would be willing to make the silent interpretation, "I'm starting to feel angry because she's rejecting me for sexual love. I could get even with her by rejecting her through a comment or two on her weight but that would only make things worse. I believe that she is actually afraid I'll reject her rather than that she is rejecting me." How would that be?

Henry: I guess I could do that.

Pastor: Then how might you feel?

Commentary: Notice the careful way the pastor follows up. Henry is not enthusiastic or committed when he responds, "I guess so." The follow-up invites Henry to get more clear and hopeful.

Henry: Less angry but I still would feel rejected.

Pastor: Sure. So might you then be willing to say quietly to her something like, "Okay. I sure miss being with you. Maybe tomorrow will be better for you."

Commentary: The pastor is supplying lots of suggested words here. If Henry is eager to learn, this can be productive. However, if Henry sees this as advice proving that the pastor knows more than he does, Henry will likely have a hidden motive of proving the pastor wrong. The pastor might proceed differently by asking, "So, if you were not going to comment on her weight and were going to gently encourage her to make love with you, what might you say?"

Henry: Well, yeah. I think she'd probably do better with that. Okay.

Pastor: All right, now let's see if we have clarity on your plans. As I understand it the next time your wife seems uninterested you will think something to yourself like . . .?

Commentary: The pastor is now reinforcing the learning and the commitment so that Henry will be more likely to engage in the new behavior some of the time over the next week or so. The pastor does well here to ask Henry to summarize his own commitments instead of doing that for him.

Henry: I'm starting to feel angry because she's rejecting me. If I nail her about her weight that will just make things worse. So instead, I'll just tell her that I miss her.

Pastor: Way to go! How does that feel?

Henry: Fine. Maybe it'll work.

Pastor: How about going with that for, say, two weeks, and then coming back to talk some more with me like this?

Henry: Sure.

Pastor's Silent Reflections: This man has faith. He's at worship nearly every Sunday. He's probably never prayed to God about anything sexual. Still his faith is a source of power here. I need to invite him to draw upon that resource.

Pastor: Okay. We can get that on the calendar in a minute before we stop for today. I'd like to ask you one other question today: Is there any way your faith might help you carry out the plan you have now?

Henry: I don't know. I suppose so. What do you have in mind?

Pastor: Well, I believe that God created marriage for sexual love and joy and wrestling and laughing and passion. So, I believe God will help you and your wife reach that goal. Praying about it might help.

Henry: Yeah. I need to pray about this.

Pastor: Will you pray to ask God to help you think silently as you have planned?

Henry: Sure.

Pastor: Okay. I'll pray for you over these next two weeks. Both of us can pray then, not that God will change your wife, but that you will feel God helping you restrain from making remarks about your wife's weight. Instead you will tell her that you miss sexual love with her when she is not ready. Okay?

Henry: Sure.

Commentary: Notice how the pastor invites this husband to become more and more narrowly focused. This greatly increases his power to keep to his plan. The subtle encouragement not to pray that God will change the wife is very powerful because one way Henry loses is to believe that his wife is fully responsible for their problem. Praying for himself helps him scapegoat her less severely.

Two weeks later the pastor and Henry met again. This time they were farther into the *Encounter* stage, exploring feelings, meanings, and motives. The pastor looked for more unconscious motives that might be hurting this husband's love for his wife. During this state, usually the third and fourth sessions, the pastor may consider the possibility of referral.

When the two men were comfortably seated, the pastor began, as Jesus so often did, with a question.

Pastor: How did you do on your commitment to yourself?

Commentary: Notice how the pastor does not ask anything that would mean "Did your strategy work and change your wife?" An important principle of Christian counseling is that none of us can change anyone except ourselves. Jesus loved Judas, Peter, and the rich young ruler and yet he did not change them. Peter became willing to be changed after his denial but Jesus did not or could not change Peter against his will.

Henry: Well, pretty good, I guess.

Pastor: Good for you! So, some of the time your wife noticed the different way you were treating her?

Henry: Yeah. [smiling] We got together several times.

Pastor: Wonderful! What is your plan now for relating to your wife?

Commentary: The pastor is now asking Henry to do his own work, to summarize what he is doing differently and to reaffirm his commitment. This is part of the *Disengagement* stage of Strategic Pastoral Counseling.

Henry: Oh, I'll keep on telling her I miss her and I'll not comment on her weight either. She seems to appreciate that.

Pastor: Great. You and she are living out more and more of the sexual joy God created for us in marriage. That's wonderful!

Commentary: The pastor reinforces each positive step Henry takes. He relates those steps in part to God's creation.

The two men continued to celebrate and Henry made some more plans to be gentle and affectionate with his wife in sexual matters. They decided not to schedule another counseling session at this time. Henry does not have deep insight into his unconscious motives for commenting on his wife's weight. Nor does he have deep insight into her needs to be special and affirmed by him. Still, his behavior is changed and they are happier together. There may be enough growth potential released that without professional help they will slowly improve their marriage and the maturity of their understanding of each other. These are typical considerations of Disengagement time.

Henry feels better about himself, his wife, and the pastor. He has more hope for sexual delight in his marriage. The pastor has listened, understood, not been critical, and has encouraged a specific, focused plan for improvement that Henry is now implementing. Though this work was done in only two sessions, Henry is considerably better off. It may be that in a few months he will return, perhaps with his wife, for the purpose of making several more specific and measurable changes in their sexual relationship. This is a practical example of what caring pastors can contribute to the lives of sexually troubled people.

2

Biblical Foundations
for Counseling Persons
with Sexual Problems

Now that we have looked at who we are, how we feel, and what we do when we try to help people with sexual problems, the next step is to search out the Scriptures for God's word to us about this aspect of ministry. The Bible gives us both divine wisdom and divine assurance as we care for troubled people.

First, we must consider some of the biblical foundations available to us in the Old and New Testaments. Then, drawing those passages together, we can sketch out a summary of biblical interpretations about sexuality in God's true way to life.

Old Testament Foundations

In the very beginning God created us, male and female together, in his own image (Gen. 1:26–27). Males reflect something of the divine image; females reflect something of the divine image. Together in holy marriage male and female reflect even more of God's essential being.

God is love. God forgives. God is morally responsible. God makes and keeps commitments. God celebrates the joy of life. We are created in God's image, so these qualities are within us. And these are essential qualities of holy marriage. God embodies the fruits of the Spirit (Gal. 5:22), and therefore male and female together grow in love, joy, peace, patience, and self-control. These godly qualities are nurtured in a marriage that expresses the image of God in the two partners and in their relationship.

Married people are to be fruitful and multiply (Gen. 1:28); they are to have children together. This was both a blessing given by God and a command. Notice that people were to bear children before the fall. Sexual intercourse was and is part of God's plan. The first sin was not the first human act of intercourse!

Adam and Eve were naked, ecstatic, unashamed, and not at all inhibited in their husband-wife sexuality, just as God created them (Gen. 2:22–25). This is God's design for husband and wife. In private we are to engage in mutual celebration of our love through sexual passion and orgasm in ways that are pleasurable to both partners and that build up the godliness of each person. Just like Adam and Eve, we are alive with excitement when we express our love in godly sexual joy.

The shame, embarrassment, and inhibition that we all feel to some degree about our sexual actions is not God's idea. This is the result of sin (Gen. 3:7, 10, 21). What, then, are we to do about our sexual inhibitions? We are to confess our sins and experience God's forgiveness so that we are freed to enjoy godly sexuality the way God intended—without embarrassment or shame while with our spouses. We Christians, more than any other people, are freed from our inhibitions to be with our spouses to shower together, to paint each others' bodies in playful or erotic ways, to be nude and make love outdoors in a private place, to engage in oral sex, and other such sensuous pleasures. We Christians, more than any other people, are freed from our inhibitions to speak tender words of love, to express words that convey how much we cherish or value our partner, to renew words of commitment, and to express love in ecstatic groans and sighs. Notice the last two sentences; men tend to focus on the first and women on the second. That is, men tend to focus on being freed from inhibitions for sexual play; women tend to focus on being freed for tender words of love. Because we are forgiven of our sins and restored to a place of grace, we can fulfill our sexuality in playful, erotic, sensuous, and sexy joy! Praise God for his forgiving and healing power!

The Bible uses the phrase "to know" in several different ways. In Genesis 4:1 Adam is described as "knowing" his wife; she then conceived and bore Cain. The term "to know" refers to sexual intercourse between husband and wife. The same Hebrew word is used for our knowledge of God (Hos. 2:20)! We are to know God, that is, have spiritual intercourse with him. We are to know one another, that is, have spiritual intercourse with each other. And when we come together as husband and wife in sexual intercourse, we experience "knowing" in a profound way.

As two married people develop a stronger and safer and deeper relationship, they open up more and more about their inner feelings, meanings, and motives. This is the content of heart-to-heart intimacy. And a kind of miracle occurs. As the husband listens to his wife disclose her emotions and the meanings of them, he not only understands her better; he understands himself better as he looks inward to see how he is alike and different from his wife. Likewise the wife knows herself in ever deeper ways as she listens to her husband describe his motives and emotions. Thus in holy marriage we are "soul mirrors."

In sexual love husband and wife know each other in their essence of being. Some of the most profound experiences we ever have with God are not those moments in which we are asking for something from God but rather in those moments in which we are deeply seeking to "be" with God. Mystical union with God is a joining of two people in pure being. In sexual orgasm expressed in holy marriage as a celebration of love, we come closest to being in oneness with another person.

The Old Testament teaches us much about the positive intent of God in creating us as sexual beings. The warnings about sexual misbehavior are designed to help us avoid painfully falling short of the beauty and joy God wants us to have as we celebrate our love sexually. By the spiritual discipline of going for God's beautiful way and of avoiding the sinful way, we open ourselves to the most delightful fulfillment of sexual love.

New Testament Foundations

The New Testament affirms the truths of the Old Testament and provides even more light about our sexuality. From it we can learn to live out even more the way of love.

Jesus quoted Genesis (2:42) when he declared that in marriage a man leaves his father and his mother and joins with his wife in creating a new oneness (Mark 10:7). The two become one. Christian marriage consists of two whole persons who are not desperate to be married. They marry because they want to, not because they are compulsively driven. It is no compliment when we introduce our spouse as "My better *half*." Two complete people join together in Christian marriage. "Incomplete people" become "co-dependents" or "love too much."

The two become one. There is unity but not uniformity, oneness but not sameness, and union but not co-dependency in the joining of husband and wife in Christian marriage. This act is an outward and visible sign of an inward and spiritual grace. Mates are joined in body, mind, spirit, heart, soul—and yet they are also separate beings. As they mature under the impact of their love they become more developed as individuals, not diminished.

Men and women are different both in God's genetic design and as a result of cultural influences. In marriage spouses may quarrel about these differences, wanting the other to think and feel as he or she does. In the oneness of Christian marriage the husband wants to learn feminine ways of doing and being; likewise his wife wants to learn masculine ways of acting and perceiving. Each learns skills from the other and thus becomes ever more a complete person.

The New Testament also teaches that sexual sins can be forgiven. We all fall far short of the biblical ideal. We all sin sexually every day in thought, word, and deed. We need forgiveness daily. Sexual sins are forgivable. God forgives adultery, homosexual acts, incest, and rape. So deep and wide and broad and high is the love of God that all our sins are forgivable as we turn to God in repentance (Rom. 8:38–39). God is faithful to forgive us; we need to confess (1 John 1:8–9). If anyone is in Christ he or she is a new creation; the old has passed away and the new has come (2 Cor. 5:17)—and all this is God's act.

The New Testament teaches that sexual intercourse is not something we do just with our genitals. Sexual union is deeply expressive of our relationship. If we have intercourse with a prostitute we actually join Jesus Christ to her (1 Cor. 6:15–16). What we do sexually with our bodies reflects who we are. When we sin sexually we do not just open ourselves up to bodily harm (sexually transmitted diseases) but also to harm of our marital relationship (1 Cor. 6:18).

A Partial Summation of Biblical Interpretations for Dealing with Sexual Problems

God created us male and female in his own image; therefore our sexuality is part of God's "very good" creation. We are free to be together sexually as husband and wife both for procreation and for celebration of love. Humans are the only creatures on this earth capable of sexual union throughout the hormonal cycle of the female. Clearly we are designed by God to make love mostly for the celebration of love and only rarely for conceiving a baby.

God created our sex organs, and they too reflect part of his loving image. God created the penis, clitoris, vagina, testicles, womb, semen, sperm, ovum, breasts, nipples, pubic hair, lips, tongue, eyes, and all other sexually related organs, and God's creation is good. God created sexual desire and passion and this is also part of his good work. How comfortable are you thanking God specifically for each of your sexual organs and for your sexually passionate feelings?

That God created sexuality primarily for sexual celebration of love can be seen very clearly in his creation of the clitoris. This organ has no part in reproduction or in protection from disease; it simply feels wonderful to be gently touched there. God gave women a sexual pleasure organ!

As in all of God's gifts we can use our sexuality in nonauthentic ways, that is, not in the way of the Author, God the Creator. When we have affairs or engage in sex with children or animals, we create within our own spirits a sense of alienation, guilt, and fear. Misuse of sex brings its own hurt, pain, and self-punishment. The proper use of sex gives pleasure and wholeness.

The engineers who designed our automobiles created them to move across hard surfaces such as streets. If we drive a car in a way that is contrary to the creator's design, such as attempting to drive it across a lake, we will do damage to the car and to ourselves. God's biblical warnings about sexual behavior are not designed to deny us sexual joy but to alert us to danger so that we can avoid doing harm to ourselves and others.

All sins are forgivable by God, even sexual sins. It is no sin to be sexually tempted though it is sinful to deny that we are tempted. When we confess our sins, God is faithful to his promise to forgive us and cleanse us of all sin (1 John 1:8–9).

We forgiven sinners called Christians are freed from shame, guilt, and inhibition in our sexuality. We sin against God's wonderful intent for our joy when we are prudish, inhibited, or rigidly reserved in our sexual play in marriage.

The more we realize that we live by God's grace and not by any moral merit of our own, the more free and hopeful we are for facing our own "dark side." We can admit that we are sometimes tempted to look at pornography, to commit adultery, or to engage in exhibitionistic or voyeuristic behavior. We all sometimes have an erotic rush in the presence of someone whom we find physically attractive. The more we are willing to be consciously aware of our "dark side" and to talk about that with God and with trusted friends, the less likely we will be to act out those impulses and yield to temptation. The more consciously aware we are of our "dark side" and the more at peace we are with the reality of our temptations, the more empowered we will be to listen to and care for people when they are sexually troubled.

God has created us sexually to join together in a union that did not exist before that moment. Just as a sperm and an ovum join and cannot be separated, so husband and wife form a new living union when they come together sexually. This is a union of selves (identity, heart, personhood), not just of bodies.

Children are a *further* blessing arising from sexual love; *oneness is the primary blessing when mates join themselves together.* In oneness with our spouses we become more aware of our partner, and as we make those discoveries we inevitably look into ourselves.

In union we grow and mature and become more God-like so that we have ever more to give to the oneness.

The New Testament uses several words for love that are useful for understanding some sexual problems. *Agapē* refers to a quality of love we can give strangers (Luke 10:29–37), enemies (Matt. 5:44), God, neighbors, and self. *Agapē* love has a willful, rational, and consciously directed quality. It is a deliberate self-giving (John 3:16). We can *agapē* love people of the opposite sex without feeling erotic emotions toward them.

A second term, *phileō*, refers to friendship love (John 3:35). Here there is a sharing of comaradery, joint work efforts, a history of events experienced together, and a heart-to-heart openness that leads to affection and joy. We can have *philia* love toward people of either sex without or with erotic emotions.

A third therm, *epithumia*, refers to strong desire (Luke 22:15) or lust (Rom. 6:12). This is a highly emotional aspect of love and when directed toward a person of the opposite sex will likely lead to some kind of sexually passionate feelings. This is a visceral or physical kind of love. The bodies of men do not know the difference between their wives, their daughters, or other women but the men's souls do. Likewise women may experience sexual arousal toward handsome, vital men as well as toward their husbands. These physical passions are not the essence of love, for they can quickly become lust. On the other hand, strong desire can add much to a married love rooted in *philia* and *agapē*.

A fourth word commonly used in Jesus' day, *eros*, does not occur in the New Testament. The term normally refers to self-love, self-esteem, or care for one's own welfare. We can only love our neighbor if we love ourselves, and God's forgiving love is what empowers us for genuine self-love.

Married love is shaped by all four aspects of love. The celebration of love sexually is stronger with *phileō* and *epithumia* and yet the fidelity that makes marriage possible is rooted deeply in *agapē*. With sufficient *eros* love we can dare to believe that our partner truly wants us and that the acts of passion and words of love we are about to give as parts of intercourse will be cherished by our partner.

If the Bible teaches that sexual love in marriage is so wonderfully expressive of God's creation, why has the church taken such a negative stance toward sexuality? The early church existed in a wildly promiscuous culture. Men made no sexual commitment of fidelity to their wives though wives were usually expected to be faithful. There were temple cultic prostitutes whose practices defiled both sexuality and faith. In this context asceticism was thought by many to be a pathway to spiritual purity. Then the false teaching that sex was exclusively for baby making led to much "sin" because married people kept violating this principle. That they intended to be "faithful" but could not resist sexual urges showed how powerful sexual drives were and therefore how much they had to be regulated. The more difficult sexual urges were to control, the more sinful they were assumed to be. Thus the church became increasingly negativistic about sexual love in marriage.

Infidelity divides and erodes oneness. The primary harm is not the sexual enjoyment of another partner or the offering of genitals to another; the primary damage is done to the oneness of the marriage union. Infidelity is not primarily a physical act; it is a violation of the oneness or ultimate purpose of marriage. Betrayal of commitment breaks union. Through Christian repentance and forgiveness trust can be rebuilt and out of the suffering of both partners may arise a more intimate marriage than existed before the betrayal.

Sexual desire lies in the self, not in the genitals. While sexual sins may defile the genitals in the sense of contracting sexually transmitted diseases, sexual sins always defile the self. We fall short of the beautiful godly ideal when we sin sexually. By putting our desire ahead of God's directions for us we diminish our communion with him and stir up guilt feelings and fears. We put ourselves at risk to become addicted to a sinful sexual activity when we engage in that activity more and more often. Sexual sins usually lead us to be more secretive, then to fear discovery; we thus alienate ourselves from others even more. It is just not true that "if no one knows, no one is hurt." Our very self is damaged and rendered less capable of godly sexual passion and pleasure when we sin sexually.

Sexual intercourse has no meaning except that which the two partners discern as they seek God's will through their passion. Some people are merely seeking orgasms or new partners to count as trophies. Some spouses "do their duty" rather than celebrate love. Some hope that sexual love will heal their inner child's wounds and thus crave sexual experience much like those similarly addicted to drugs. However, one way to add to the fulfillment of married sexual love is to explore with each other the meanings of that love as God has revealed them in the Scriptures and in the experience itself. When the motive for coming together is love and the celebrative intent is love, and when the physical union symbolizes a far deeper loving oneness of spirit, then sexual intercourse is filled with meaning and joy!

Another inspiring insight of Scripture that can help us deal with our sexuality is the divinely revealed truth that love is a motive, a reason why we do what we do. First Corinthians 13:1–4 clearly teaches that when we do godly things for ungodly motives we accomplish no good. When we do what we do as we are empowered or motivated by godly love, we fulfill God's beautiful creativity within us, and the outcome is lovely and exciting.

Is masturbation sinful? The answer to this question may depend upon the motivation of the person. If a wife just had a baby, the husband may masturbate to relieve sexual pressures in ways that do not violate their relationship. If a wife is learning to be orgasmic and uses masturbation to help her tune in to her body and her feelings so that she can have godly ecstasy with her husband, surely she is not sinning. The motives of these two people are love. On the other hand, consider the person who masturbates while having a sexual fantasy about someone at work or in church; that is lust (Matt. 5:28) and is a rehearsal of adultery, making that more likely to occur.

Motivation is a profound part of being sexually authentic. Sometimes when a married couple is engaging in sexual intercourse the wife is doing this to appease the husband so he won't be angry or so he will agree to buy a better car for her. Suppose the husband wants release for himself whether his wife is willing or not. At other times this couple may be motivated by godly love to celebrate the love they share in marriage—willful and deliberate, friendly and affectionate, passionate and full of strong desire, and each with a self-love that makes self-giving a key aspect of their sexual experience. As we work with people who tell us about their sexual problems, let us listen carefully for both stated and hidden motives and then help them learn to be more and more motivated by love.

The Scriptures provide us with godly foundations for doing our counseling work with sexually troubled people. The Christian faith helps us know the truth of the authentic way to life in sexually passionate love making in marriage. The Christian faith helps us receive forgiveness over and over as we inevitably sin sexually. As repentant and forgiven Christians we know the truth and are set free to celebrate marital love in sexually passionate, playful, and sensuous ways—just as God intended!

3

Specific Aspects of the Pastoral Counseling Relationship

W e have described pastoral principles for a counseling ministry and have summarized some biblical foundations for helping people with sexual problems. We can now move to consideration of vital and specific aspects of our counseling conversations. Whatever the problem and whoever the pastor, part of what the pastor does is listen compassionately, stay alert to dangerous distortions, and respond with helpful biblical wisdom and love. Here are some practical applications of those principles.

Fundamental Relationship Skills

In pastoral counseling of five sessions or less, you as pastor have the opportunity to care for people in a truly gospel-directed manner full of love and hope and grace. In turning to you with sexual problems, counselees have very likely overcome much initial embarrassment and fear. As you gather in Jesus' name, he will be with you (Matt. 18:20) for healing and learning as you apply the gospel to problems in human sexuality.

When the individual shows up for the first counseling session, there will be a definite need to reshape your relationship for this kind of personal work. Some people will come expecting the pastor to chastise them. Most will unconsciously assume that the pastor will relate to them about sex as their parents did years before. Some will idealize the pastor and then feel deeply disappointed when the pastor inevitably does not fulfill that ideal. Whenever the person responds inappropriately with emotions that are either illogical in content or surprisingly intense, the pastor needs to recognize that an unconscious distortion of the relationship is occurring. If that cannot be worked through directly, referral is in order. We will make specific suggestions about how to do this later in this chapter.

Within the framework of brief Strategic Pastoral Counseling, we present some specifics that enhance this intrinsically spiritual relationship.

First, ask questions that can best be answered by descriptive language. Questions like "How long have you been married?" can be answered briefly and factually and may not reveal much that is of use. A question that invites description may be more helpful: "What usually happens when you two talk at home about this problem?"

Most of us respond defensively to questions that begin with "Why." "Why" questions stir up feelings in many people that are linked to childhood when mother may have exclaimed, "*Why* did you spill your milk?" "*Why* don't you pray about it?" "*Why* is your wife saying 'No' to sex with you?" We can ask "What might be some reasons your wife . . . ?" Or, "How come your husband . . . ?"

Second, listen for feelings, meanings, and motives more than for facts, errors, and logical solutions. If a husband exclaims with an edge in his voice, "We haven't had sex in two months!" a pastoral response might be, "That must be frustrating for you!" The pastor expresses both understanding and support for this husband's pain by use of the word "frustrating." This might be followed up by asking another question: "What is your best understanding about the reasons you two are not having sex now?"

Third, as people explain the problem, deal with generalities by responding with questions that invite them to be more specific. This helps people focus on manageable "chunks" of the overall problem. Wife: "He touches me in ways I don't like." Pastor: "What is his response when you tell him specifically what you do not like?"

Fourth, when a person pours out the presenting problem and seems to relax after reaching that point, ask, "What possible constructive steps have you thought of so far?" If we move too quickly to the generating of solutions, the individual may feel like we do not care enough to take time to listen and understand. Sometimes the person will indicate readiness to consider options by stating, "So, that's about it. I just don't know what to do. I've thought about going to the doctor to see if there is something wrong with me, hormones or something." We can respond by affirmation: "That may be quite helpful. And what other options do you have?"

Fifth, a powerful resource for hope and creativity in generating options is the use of Scripture with people who are open to that. When we are in the understanding mode, we are wise to say little except, "Please go on," or "Tell me more," and to ask questions that invite further sharing. Bringing in Scripture too soon will seem like a quick and easy answer to many people, and they will likely feel rejected. Once they have described the problem we can ask, "How might God be helping you with this problem?" "Who in the Bible wrestled with a problem similar to yours? How did God help him (her)?" "What Bible verse might give you hope for a solution?"

If the person seems to want biblical help and yet does not come up with something specific, you might want to offer a tentative possibility for him or her. "As I hear about your stress and hurt I think about 2 Timothy 1:7, which encourages us with these words: 'God did not give us a spirit of timidity, but a spirit of power, of love and of self-discipline.' How might that verse be of help to you now?" Notice how the use of the question puts the work right back on the individual. If we are conveying unconditional love or grace so that this person feels safe, he or she may just say, "Oh, I suppose that is true and it should help me, but I still feel discouraged." At that point we do well to drop the verse and go back to compassionate listening.

"You feel so discouraged that it's hard to get going with much hope for change, is that it?" If the person then exclaims, "I have resolved time and time again to break this filthy habit, but I keep slipping back into it!" we might then ask, "Will you please tell me step by step what happened the last time you had a slip back into this habit?" By asking for specifics, we help the person gain more focus; in this situation, the focus is on the way he or she slips back into a hurtful habit.

Sixth, after we have listened and understood, we are sometimes in a position to make tentative suggestions as to how this person might begin to resolve the problem. Some secular counselors do not believe in this approach while others do. The concern is that instead of tentative suggestions we may impose advice to unconsciously meet our own need to feel wise or superior. However, in the Christian faith the basic principle is to make suggestions in a spirit of love and respect for the other person without trying to impose solutions.

If we have listened to a husband talk about how other women come on to him but his wife won't, we may begin to understand him. He may be attempting to cover his own inadequacy by implying there must be something wrong with his wife. He may be delivering a subtle threat that if she doesn't come around soon, he may take the offer of one of these other women. His wife may be so hurt by this that she isn't emotionally interested in sexual love with her husband.

Under these circumstances what Christian behavior might you suggest to this husband? We do have help to give him. We might explain, "Now that I have heard how tough the problem is, I want to make several suggestions and ask you to consider them, okay? First, I believe that you love your wife and that in your heart you know that talking about these other women is hurtful and unloving. I suggest that you not bring up the other women again. My second suggestion is that you think in courtship terms of thoughtful, affectionate, romantic actions you can take to let your wife know you love her. My last suggestion is that you make these changes without any expectation that she will quickly change and become sexually responsive to you. These changes would then be loving and not manipulative. Now, what do you feel in your heart as I encourage you to consider these steps?" We then listen carefully to see if the counselee is immediately resistant, is considering the possibility, or needs to revise the suggestions before committing to them. We should not impose our solution on the counselee; that, too, would be unloving and would be analogous to the way the husband is treating his wife!

Finally, think "referral" when appropriate. By cultivating relationships with other professionals who have expertise in areas sometimes needed by people you counsel, you will be more likely to think about referral when you need to. Some people need a physician to determine if there are organic causes of their problem. Others need intensive psychotherapy requiring more counselor time and training than all but a very few pastors have. Being aware of and comfortable with our creaturely limits helps all of us think about referral as we listen to people.

The Ministry of Referral

In talking with counselees about referral, we need to convey our continuing concern so that they will not feel rejected or abandoned. We can explain, "I am glad you sought me out and I thank you for trusting me enough to share your problems with me. I know someone, a Christian, in our city who has special training in the area of your need. I want to introduce you to that person and see if you can gain further help there. This person is licensed as a sex therapist [or other] and works in an office building near here. His [her] name is_____. What I would like to do is call him and describe your situation and then get back to you and have you call for an appointment. If that is okay, then after you have seen him, I would want to talk with him and with you about how I may continue to be helpful until you have solved this problem. Is that okay? What questions do you have?"

As we describe specific counseling scenes in the chapters that follow, we will provide more dialogue examples that will help make these counseling skills more explicit. This brief summary and the case examples in this chapter are designed to provide an opportunity for you to gain a more thorough understanding of your counseling relationship with people.

Privacy and Confidentiality in Pastoral Counseling

To be effective in loving God's people through the special ministry of the counseling relationship, we need to think about privacy and confidentiality. We need to have nearly sound-proof offices. We need to minimize interruptions by the telephone or the church secretary. We need to keep our commitment to maintain in confidence whatever is shared with us unless we obtain written permission or unless we are in professional consultation with another person as a part of our care for the counselee (clinical supervision; physician consultation on medications).

We also need to be careful to spell out in the first session the limits of confidentiality according to the laws of the state in which we serve. Even ordained ministers do not have the power to keep everything in confidence. You need to find out the limits of confidentiality for ministers in your state.

Listening to the Client

As we listen to an individual describe a sexual problem, we do well to gather some factual data. We will probably need to know how long the problem has persisted, what was going on in the person's life when the problem began (some men begin an affair when they are depressed over failures at work), and other sources of help that have been sought (other counselors; a physician). We may need to ask how long this person has been married and if this is a first marriage. If this is not a first marriage we will probably want to know how the current problem was dealt with in the previous marriage(s).

Though we need factual data in order to develop a framework of understanding, we do well to listen at a far deeper level to what counselees are saying. Listen for feelings, meanings, and motives. As we listen at this level we will learn much about the inner workings of this individual's personality as he or she attempts to cope with the problem at hand. The issue is not so much what kind of problem this person has as what kind of person has this problem. So we do well to understand the person who has the problem first, then look at the problem itself.

Feelings or emotions may range from rage to depression to excitement to lust to sorrow to nostalgia to regret to hope to joy. We do well to ask people how they feel about their problem. Answers such as "Okay," "Better," "Not okay," or "Worse" are neither descriptive nor revealing. We can follow up such answers with a question such as, "Well, what I mean is, what emotions such as mad, sad, and glad do you feel?"

Then we will be wise to tune in to the meanings the emotions have for the individual. One way to get at meaning is to think in terms of how this person feels about feeling this way. We always have feelings about feelings! If men look at a magazine full of photographs of nude women, they will feel some level of sexual arousal. How do we feel about being sexually aroused? We may feel guilty or embarrassed or excited.

We can ask, "You feel discouraged because—?" The client may further elaborate: "Because I have been seeing you each week trying to figure out what to do and I still feel stuck." Now we may begin to grasp more of the person's pain. Perhaps he is blaming us because he has been seeing us weekly and isn't any better. Perhaps he is blaming himself for being a slow learner. We can ask, "What is your hunch about why you are still stuck even though you have been seeing me each week for help?"

Another level of listening and understanding is to listen for the motives underlying feelings and meanings. One of the most brilliant revelations in Scripture is the teaching that love is a motive (1 Cor. 13:1–4). All our behavior is motivated by love—even our sinful, self-defeating behavior. If a man yells at his wife, "Get off my back!" he may actually be feeling deep down inside, "If you really loved me you would stop criticizing me and would give me a compliment about what I do right." We strongly encourage you to continually ask yourself silently, "How might this person be attempting to give or receive love through this logically self-defeating behavior?" By discerning effort from this perspective you will truly "listen" to people at a deeper level.

Another way of describing what we have shared thus far in this section about listening is to say: "Process is more important than content." When we are listening to troubled people, *how* they are responding to their troubles (process or method used) is more of a problem than the actual problem (content). So if Harry is a forty-five-year-old who has been working eighty hours per week for months because of a decrease in his company's market share, his wife may feel rejected and hurt (process). If he gets angry at her for feeling hurt (process), she may feel even more hurt (process). The content may be that they only make love about once a month. If we focus on that as if it were the problem, there will be little improvement in their relationship or their sex life.

Most of us have also learned to listen to the nonverbal messages in communications. Some of the main nonverbal clues are voice tone (an angry edge or sad plea), rate of speech, volume, body posture (such as rigidity, arms folded across the chest, or slumped, looking at the floor) and behaviors such as being early or late for appointments, "forgetting" counseling homework commitments, or choice of seat in your office (near the door, across from your desk, alongside you).

Jesus asked people questions and listened to their direct (verbal) and their implied (nonverbal) answers. He listened for the "heart message" or the deep meaning rather than just the stated message. When a man asked Jesus, "Good teacher, what must I do to inherit eternal life?" Jesus responded with "Why do you call me good?" Jesus intuited that the man did not truly think Jesus was good. Perhaps Jesus heard a sarcastic tone in the man's voice. Perhaps there was a frown on his face or his hands were doubled into fists. Because Jesus truly "heard" this man, they continued in dialogue instead of just debating a doctrine (Mark 10:17).

As followers of Christ we listen to people as a way of expressing our love for them in God's name. The Holy Spirit will bless our listening by giving us discernment about what is truly going on and then helping us know what words to say (Luke 12:12).

The Sexually Seductive Counselee

Most pastors have had someone "come on" to them and know what a dangerous and complex experience that can be. Talking privately with people about very intimate sexual needs and frustrations is an extraordinary opening for temptation for both the pastor and the counselee. If we are not careful, we may end up violating our faith and our ordination. We may get into an affair, a scandal, and a malpractice lawsuit!

The most common motive for being seductive toward the pastor is not a complimentary and loving one at all. Many women who have been sexually abused by their fathers will come on sexually to the male "father figure" represented by the pastor. This is a clear transference of feelings from father to pastor. What the person is expressing is desire for fatherly love and hatred for not receiving that; she is not expressing love!

One woman who had successfully seduced her previous pastor-counselor told me, "I knew he was trash if he would go to bed with a woman like me!" Clearly for her, seducing the pastor was a hostile act much as is the case with a male rapist. She was destroying a man who represented her father who had sexually abused her for years.

Another motive for seductive behavior is similar to that of hidden hostile attack. This person has a motive of wanting to make a conquest. Seducing the pastor means winning another "trophy." Since the "victor" has enticed the pastor to act against his faith, this means that the seducer must be especially powerful and desirable. People who are motivated in this fashion are usually narcissistic individuals who glory in the control of others in order to reassure themselves that they are not the shame-based people they unconsciously believe they are.

Excessively dependent people often behave seductively toward the pastor. Such troubled individuals may see the pastor as a kind of hero and fantasize that if they could only have a relationship with such a fine person that would make them okay. Dependent people can invite caretaking so subtly that the pastor is at first unconsciously drawn into a rescuer role and then becomes a willing sexual partner.

We pastors must be very clear in our hearts and minds that when someone behaves seductively toward us he or she is *never* showing us authentic love. That person may adore us or be "in love" with us but that is not love. This seductiveness is based upon illusion, transference, hostility, and dependency, not willful self-giving for mutual growth in godliness. Since the two people involved both know this behavior is sinful and destructive they cannot be motivated by genuine love if they move ahead together.

The most powerful way to deal with our own emotional needs as we hear people discuss their sexuality is through confession. We need to have a confidant, a professional Christian counselor or another pastor, to whom we disclose that while listening to a counselee we became sexually excited and asked for more intimate details than we needed, or, we became fearful and shut off the talk. If we confess our faults to one another and pray for one another, we can be healed (James 5:16).

One minister was seeing a sexually promiscuous woman who presented many details about her sex life. He became sexually excited at times in his sessions with her. One day, when she was scheduled to come in, the pastor began to fantasize that she would come in wearing a long coat and that when she took it off she would be nude. He immediately called another pastor and told him about these feelings. As he spoke, the feelings subsided. The pastor asked his friend to pray for him during the counseling hour. When the woman came in, the pastor told her about his fantasy and the control steps he had taken. She wept with relief and went on to grow much.

Some Do's and Don'ts in
Helping with Sexual Problems

Do give love and encouragement. Do pray with people after learning what kind of prayer they most want. Do teach them what the Bible says about meanings and values in human sexuality. Do help people connect at deeper and deeper levels their sexuality and their love of God, neighbor, and self. Do refer them to Christian professional psychotherapists if they have not made substantial progress in four or five sessions. Do follow up a few weeks later with them to see how they are doing with the referral counselor.

Don't ignore your own sexual needs as you work with these hurting people. Do get your sexual needs met outside the counseling session in responsible ways. Your temptation to use clients to get your needs met is thereby sharply reduced.

Don't give answers or solutions such as, "I can't tell you what to do but if it were me I would . . ." Don't focus on facts and logic; do focus on feelings, meanings, and motives. Don't violate commitments of confidentiality. Don't probe or pressure people to share more of the details of their sexual problems with you; ask gently and then let them set the pace for such intimate disclosures.

Don't try to change the person. Jesus could not change the rich young ruler or Judas. We cannot change anyone but ourselves. We can show people how to change themselves but we cannot change them. We have not failed if they do not change; they have chosen not to change. If we give hope and love and some useful information, they may decide they can change and do so.

An Example of Christian Counseling

As you read the pastor's words in the dialogue below, please listen to your own inner being. Would you have responded the same way? Why or why not? As you read each client statement, frame your response before you read the pastoral response, then compare. What about you prompted you to choose a different approach? As you read the pastor's silent reflections become aware of what you would be feeling and thinking in that situation. Read the commentary section for additional information about counseling strategy.

A married couple had great difficulty having sexual joy in their marriage and they approached the pastor about it. After listening for fifteen minutes or so, the pastor had a hunch that both these people mismanaged anger often. They were so frequently angry that their readiness for sexual love was greatly diminished. He also decided to simplify the dialogue by talking with Karen while Bob listened and then switching to Bob as Karen listened.

Pastor:	Bob, will it be okay with you if I ask Karen questions as you listen and then after ten minutes or so talk with you the same way?
Bob:	Sure.
Pastor:	Thank you. [turning toward Karen] Is that okay with you, Karen?
Karen:	Yes.
Pastor:	Well, Karen I think it would help me understand your problem if you would answer this question: How did your parents get along when you were a child at home?
Karen:	Okay. They quarreled, but doesn't everybody? [laughs]
Pastor:	What did they say and do when they quarreled?
Karen:	Well . . . usually Mother would say something like, 'George, how many times do I have to tell you to take out the garbage? It looks to me like you could see that for yourself.' Dad would reply, 'Oh, get off my back. I'm doing it now.' Then they wouldn't say much to each other for an hour or so.
Pastor:	Did they have cool periods like that daily or weekly or what?
Karen:	Oh, several times a week, sometimes more, I suppose.
Pastor:	And how often do you and Bob get cool like that?
Karen:	Every day or so, now that I think about it.
Pastor:	I imagine that cuts into your ability to play with each other and celebrate sexual love.
Karen:	I guess it does. When we are irritated with each other we just sort of keep a distance. Then, without saying anything, we just sort of pretend nothing has happened and get back together. I like sex and love and . . . I think Bob and I do . . . uhhh . . . okay in bed, but we're missing out somehow on the joy of being married.
Pastor:	What is joyful for you about sexual love with Bob?
Karen:	Oh . . . it feels good to be close like that. . . . Touched, satisfied, relaxed . . . just . . . together.
Pastor:	Sounds like your parents all over again.
Karen:	What's *that* supposed to mean?

Pastor's Silent Reflections: What happened? She's angry as if I am accusing her of something. Slow down! I was too quick with that last remark.

Commentary: The pastor's question, "What is joyful for you about sexual love with Bob?" could mean to Karen that he is asking about specific sexual acts in which they engage. He has not prepared their relationship for such an intimate question. Probably the main source of Karen's irritation is his comment, "Sounds like your parents all over again." This interpretation leaps far ahead of where Karen is thirty minutes into the first counseling session. The pastor may be applying an important psychological principle and yet is doing so too soon for Karen. He may also be hearing Karen's words "satisfied, relaxed, together" and feel that they do not sound passionate and orgasmic to him. He may have let a male bias creep in here.

Pastor: I regret that my comment was hurtful. Part of my understanding is that usually in marriage we all unconsciously repeat patterns of relationships that we observed in our parents as we grew up. I think I see something of that here and yet I think I moved too quickly into the idea. Do you have questions you need to ask me to clarify anything about our counseling relationship?

Karen: No.

Pastor: Do you need something from me now that would help you be more ready to be open with me?

Commentary: The pastor is not defensive. He does not give a long explanation for why he said what he did. He is not critical of Karen for her tenseness. He is patiently acknowledging his error and inviting her to improve her relationship with him. This is a deeply important learning experience for Karen. She and the pastor had a conflict and they used a method quite different from her parents' style to deal with it. They did not remain angry and stop talking at a cool distance. They are working through their problem now, living out in the counseling session a new way of relating for Karen.

Karen: I trust you. I just didn't understand where you were coming from. What is the parallel that you see?

Pastor: That your parents were okay people and yet when they got angry at each other they clammed up instead of talking it through. This may have led them to a more laid-back style and perhaps to a joylessness in much of their sexual loving.

Karen: Oh, I don't know.

Pastor: Perhaps I've misunderstood something important here. I regret that. I'd like to correct my misimpression. Will you tell me what kind of play your parents did with each other when you were little? Can you imagine your mother and your father laughing, giggling, and playing sexually in bed? Did your parents go on vacations together alone while leaving you with your grandparents?

Commentary: **The pastor is hurrying here, trying to make his point so that Karen will see that he does have an important contribution to make. Asking a string of questions without waiting for answers usually hinders the flow of communication. Still, his Christian care for Karen is more powerful for her than his style of the moment.**

Karen: No. None of that happened in our home. So you think my home wasn't normal?

Pastor: Sounds as if there was much love, commitment, and work, but not a lot of joy, play, or sexual passion and there was a lot of silent anger. You may have just absorbed a view like that from them, and perhaps unconsciously now relate to Bob the same way.

Karen: Gee . . . that sounds like I'm stuck in my ways. Is there any hope? [smiling]

Pastor: Yes, by the power of God, you can make a commitment to discover new joy in your marriage and if Bob is willing to work to understand both you and himself, you two can develop some new patterns in your marriage relationship. For example, can you think of a woman friend here at church that you believe is probably very sexy, joyful, and playful with her husband?

Karen: Yes.

Pastor: Will you talk with her and find out how she feels, how she frees herself up to be that way? Then ask her how she and her husband work through their angry spells.

Karen: Yeah, I'll do that.

Pastor: Good for you. Now, Karen, if this feels like a good place, I'd like to talk with Bob some and when we finish I'll ask you and him if you are ready to make a prayerful commitment here today to go for joy, play, and sexiness with each other. Okay?

Karen   Sure.

Pastor: Bob, are you willing to think out loud with me and tell me what you understand about Karen's problems, from her point of view?

Bob: Sure. I know her parents and they are good people and yet like she says they are not much into fun and games. Her mother pouts and her father goes out into the garage a lot by himself just to get away.

Pastor: And how might growing up with them have affected Karen?

Bob: She's probably absorbed a lot from them, become like them. She pouts with me. In spite of myself I go out in the backyard and work when I'm angry at her. I don't want to blame her parents, but they didn't know much about having fun or getting over being angry.

Pastor: Good for you, not to blame them. Instead of blaming, we can learn from the past about why we are the way we are today. Okay, so what does Karen need from you?

Bob: Understanding? Help? But when I try to get her to be playful she just doesn't seem to be interested.

Pastor: How do you try?

Bob: I ask her to loosen up, get with it. I bought her a sexy nightgown and she won't even wear it. I got a copy of *The Joy of Sex* and she seemed embarrassed by the pictures . . . never read it . . . I'm frustrated. A man's got needs!

Pastor's Silent Reflections: Bob's having difficulty tuning in to Karen's needs. His efforts to invite her to be playful sound critical and self-oriented. That probably hurts Karen even more. Change directions for a while.

Pastor: I can imagine at times that you feel like climbing a wall! If you are willing now I'd like to know what parallels you see in your relationship with Karen and your parents' style when you were a boy.

Bob: Well, my parents were quite different from hers. My dad worked long hours and Mother pretty much had the load at home all on herself with my two brothers and myself. When Dad came home he tended to give orders, be angry and tense and tired. He never hit us or anything . . . he was just angry much of the time. Mother didn't fight with him, she just sort of . . . seemed to go along with him and yet eventually she usually got her way somehow.

Pastor: So, do you treat Karen in some ways similar to the ways your parents treated each other?

Bob: Well, I guess I get angry, frustrated . . . she'd say "critical." Then I get frustrated even more when she clams up, sort of like Mother.

Pastor: So it may be that you are ready to commit to not using anger and criticism to try to get what you want from Karen, to not blame either her or yourself, and instead get on with "putting away childish things" as 1 Corinthians 13 reminds us, and building with her the kind of marriage you both want instead of modeling the style of marriage you each observed as children.

Bob: I'd like that. I feel some hope now. I never thought of it this way before—that we are doing things to each other just because we saw our parents do it that way! We don't have to continue to copy our parents where we don't want to.

Pastor: Right! So, let's stop there for today and meet again in two weeks and see just how much you both have gained in insight and power to change these childhood patterns. That will be difficult at first. If two weeks from now you think you need more intensive help, I can refer you to a friend of mine who specializes in marriage counseling. If you talk several times a week about your anger and open up about what you want, you probably won't need that kind of help.

Commentary: Here the pastor is both setting the stage for referral, if needed, and subtly giving Karen and Bob some additional motivation to work on their relationship. If they work they can avoid the expense in time and money of professional marriage counseling. When he declares, "That will be difficult at first," he is alerting them to the difficulty of what they are undertaking. He is clear that he does not expect that all their problems will be solved in two weeks.

Pastor: Are you ready to make prayerful commitments? Karen, are you ready to talk out your anger with Bob and then be playful and joyful in sexiness with him?

Karen: Yes! I am.

Pastor: Great! And you, Bob, will you playfully ask Karen for what you want and not use angry criticism to try to get what you want?

Bob: Sure.

Pastor: Then let's join hands and pray together. Suppose I open the prayer and then you both declare to God whatever your personal commitments are and then I'll close the prayer. Okay?

Responding with Compassion, Suggestions, and Hope

We listen. We ask questions about feelings, meanings, and motives so that we can understand at deeper and deeper levels. We listen to our own inner being as we hear what people say. Eventually we truly understand in compassionate ways what this human being is experiencing. On this basis we can make specific suggestions or teach life management skills that may be practical and helpful to our clients. As we relate in compassion, understanding, and practical suggestions, and as we do this with in-spired ("in the Spirit") warmth, people gain hope that they can change.

Part 2

Applications
Specific Sexual Problems and Christian Responses

4

Gender Differences
in Resolving Sexual Problems

Many of the sexual and relational problems people bring to us
are exacerbated by a misunderstanding of gender differences.
Henry Higgins was neither the first nor the last man to cry out, "Why
can't a woman be like a man!" Modern women sigh in exasperation
when they declare, "Men just *don't* get it!"

From the perspective of Christian theology male and female
together reflect the image of God. In marriage male and female
come together to form a oneness. This oneness is an integration
that enables us to relate well through the appreciation and then
application of our differences. Oneness is made physically clear in
the sexual union we can achieve because of our genital differences.

Some of our differences seem to be biologically influenced; others are probably culturally conditioned. Though our patterns of
relationship are *influenced* by biology, our behavior is not *caused*
by biology. Created in the image of God, we have will and choice
in how we express our biological condition and energies.

There is another important consideration in thinking about gender-related issues. Sociological data about how we behave can tell

us a lot about how one hundred randomly selected men or women will respond to a stimulus. Such data tell us nothing, however, about how a particular person will respond. That is, while men will have some gender-related tendencies to behave in a certain manner, all men will not behave that way and some women may exhibit that same behavior. Scientific data do not support overgeneralized statements about "all men" or "all women."

Some Relational Gender Differences

Women seem to be able to utilize their left brain and right brain in tandem whereas men are more lateralized. There are actually more neuron connections between the two brain hemispheres in women than in men. Therefore many men want to "focus" and concentrate whereas many women can do two or three things well at the same time.

Women tend to be more compliant to rules than men.

Most females, at any age, are more nurturant than most males.

Most males respond best to positive cues and encouragement while most females respond best to critical cues and corrections.

Among children, males are more exploratory, adventuresome, and inclined to risk taking than females. Males are more inclined to value freedom, independence, and competition and seem to need to prove themselves by being daring. Whereas men tend to be aggressive and to penetrate, women tend to receive, shelter, and protect. Women are more likely to be cautious and security-oriented. Most women tend to value love, harmony, beauty, and cooperation in community.

Most women are superior to men in hearing acuity, and most men are superior to women in visual acuity.

Most males have more difficulty enhancing their masculinity than females have in developing their femininity. For females, femininity is a continuation of their relationship with their primary source, mother. For boys, developing masculinity means defining and declaring how they are different from mother. Most men fear lack of achievement. Most women fear lack of relationship.

Men tend toward task orientation and may lose sight of the needs of the people involved in the task. Women tend to take care that the people involved in the task enjoy themselves and don't get hurt; the task is secondary.

Women tend to experience their emotions with more intensity or biological reaction and thus may appear to many men as out of control when they show strong feelings. Women tend to have more mood fluctuations than men. When women assess men in feminine terms, men may seem to be cool, indifferent, and uncaring. When men assess women in masculine terms, women may seem to be unstable and often out of control emotionally.

Women tend to have many more friends with whom they confide than do men.

Girls tend to speak at an earlier age than boys and to have larger vocabularies. Parents tend to talk more with female children. Males may avoid something which they are not perceived as skilled for and therefore relate more with actions than through words.

Women tend to need lots of support when engaging in outward-directed growth and risk taking. Women tend to be more skilled and comfortable when engaged in inward-directed growth. Conversely, men tend to need lots of support when engaging in inward-directed growth (such as in the counseling relationship or in marital dialogue) and to be much more comfortable taking on an outward-directed task.

Men tend to identify themselves by what they *do*. Men do not tend to think about their marriage when at work. Career achievement is the high goal though work may be conceptualized as a sacrificial task made for the good of the family. Women tend to identify themselves by stating with whom they are related, who they *are*. Women often put marriage and children first, career success second. Thus when there is a marital difficulty, men tend to want to *do something* external such as fix the leaky faucet or change the car's oil. In such circumstances women tend to go inward and search for how they can *relate* better in order to improve the situation.

Because masculinity is traditionally defined by separation, the husband is threatened by intimacy. Likewise, since femininity is defined by relations, the wife is threatened by isolation.

Faced with a choice, women tend to look for a solution that will hurt the fewest people and create the most positive feelings. Men tend to look for a solution based upon fairness or some other similar abstract principle.

There is more social pressure on women to be thin than there is on men to be trim. In most cultures, there is more pressure on women to be mothers than there is on men to be fathers.

When talking intimately about heartfelt matters, most men seem to want some structure, some agreements or assurances as to how the two will talk in order to feel safe and open to self-disclosure. Men may ask for a time limit and a topic limit. Many women report that setting up such structure makes them feel that the man does not want to talk with them in loving, sharing ways.

When husband and wife talk, women are the most likely to ask questions; men are more likely to interrupt. The women then complain, "He never listens!" When he is talking and she nods her head, he interprets that body language to mean that she agrees; she intends to convey that she is listening, not necessarily agreeing. Most women seem to believe that talking about their marital relationship is part of the joy of living. Many men tend to think that if a relationship is working, there is no need to talk about it. Or if his wife wants to talk about their relationship, the husband quickly assumes that something must be wrong.

No wonder we have so many sexual difficulties and so much stress as we attempt to work out our sexual problems! We Christians have the same difficulties to face as others; but we also have marvelous help from God for learning and growing and working through these problems.

Gender Differences Affecting Sexual Problems

The biggest sexual differences between males and females are not genital but have to do with how we go about being sexual. Men, generally, are more excited about what they see and thus many husbands buy their wives very sexy negligees and are frustrated when their wives won't wear them. Men generally hunger more for variety of sexual practices than do most women. Women often hunger for variety of mood and atmosphere and then feel sexually used when their husbands seem to only want one thing in sex.

Most women want words of love, affection, and appreciation and want to know that they are cherished as part of love making. Most men fear that words will somehow ruin the love-making session.

Many men, younger men in particular, are very quick to arousal and move too fast (from their wives' perspective) to genital touching and intercourse. Older men get keyed up more slowly and thus tend to better match the arousal rate of their wives.

Many men have a tendency toward keeping account records about sex. They may read in the newspapers that the average couple has intercourse 2.3 times per week. They immediately tally their own sexual activity and feel frustrated if their figure is "only" two times per week. Men may read that many women are capable of multiple orgasms and then want to make that a goal to be reached in their next love-making session. Most women find this counting to be strange, even demeaning to women or a demand for genital sex rather than a desire for a personal love relationship.

Husbands tend to believe that they have somehow failed their wives if they do not "give" them an orgasm. For most men orgasm is the highest point of love making and to "fail" to have an orgasm is a big loss. Therefore many husbands believe that they have not been sexy enough when their wives do not have orgasmic climax each time. Actually a husband cannot "give" his wife an orgasm. He can help her give herself one, or she can block herself from having an orgasm no matter what he does.

Most wives want to be pursued and see husbandly pursuit as an expression of their attractiveness. Therefore a wife may be disappointed if her husband comes on to her just a bit and then backs off if she does not immediately say "Yes." What she often wants is for him to wait a few minutes and then approach her again in a different manner. She then starts to feel a beginning level of thrill such that she wants to make love. She has "gotten in the mood" in response to his pursuit.

Many couples seen in counseling report a paradox in that the husband declares that he wishes his wife would initiate love making once in a while. The wife often responds that she is the only one who suggests love making now. How can two married people arrive at such opposite interpretations of their experience with each other? He may be counting as invitations to love making such expressions as, "How about we get to bed a little early tonight?" She may see little love, desire, or sexual passion in such words and therefore not see this as an attempt to initiate love making. She may shower, brush her teeth, fix her hair, and put on a nice robe and then go to the room where her husband is. He may speak to her and then begin to caress her and believe that he initiated love making because he began the first sexual action. For her, preparing her body was a sensuous step and going to where he was wearing nothing but her robe was a blatant invitation.

A common thread throughout most of these differences and complaints is fear of rejection. The husband does not give her the words of love she most wants to hear for fear she will laugh at him for his poor choice of words or will respond by telling him that the words are nice but she needs to hear such talk more often. The husband does not boldly pursue his wife in a playful manner for fear she will know exactly what he is up to and will refuse him. The wife may fear to playfully touch her husband or to show off her body to him in the belief she is not attractive enough or that her genital touches will only make him hunger for sex, not her. Our fear of rejection inhibits us from many wonderful moments of sexual love making and celebration of Christian marital oneness.

Pastoral Counseling Through Gender Difference Problems

The pastor had performed the wedding ceremony for Walter and Tina. They had been married six years and had one child about four years of age. They were seated in the pastor's office. Tina was weeping softly. Walter was tense and stern.

Tina: I'm sorry . . .

Pastor: Feel your feelings. You're okay.

Tina: Well, we're just not getting along much. I know Walt loves me, but I don't feel loved, you know what I mean?

Pastor: Is it that you are confident that he loves you in the sense that he cares about your well-being and safety but he doesn't seem to be excited about you?

Tina:	Yes! He says I don't like sex, but I do! I just want him to want me!
Pastor:	Walt, how do you see the problem between Tina and yourself?
Walter:	I do love her, but she is busy with work and Kara [their four-year-old] and she has little time for me. We only have sex about once a month now.
Pastor:	Are you willing to talk about increasing your sexual love with Tina?

Commentary: The pastor has chosen to move from the *Encounter* stage to the *Engagement* stage in counseling. Though he has only been talking with this couple for perhaps fifteen minutes, he does know them from being with them often at church activities. He senses that they trust him. He is now asking them to decide on some focus for their counseling work.

Walter:	Sure . . . if she is.
Pastor:	Tina?
Tina:	Yes. That's why I am here.
Pastor:	Good. Thank you both. Now you have a focus for dialogue. Each of you is willing to change to increase your sexual love play with each other. Walt, what might you be willing to change about yourself, if Tina thought she would like the change?
Walter:	I don't know. It's hard to say. I just want to . . . uhhh . . . do it more often, you know?
Pastor:	Yes. Love making once a month is hardly likely to bring much joy to your marriage. If you were to decide to initiate love making with Tina once a week, what assurances would you want from her to help you want to reach out to her that way?
Walter:	I'd . . . uhhh . . . want to know that she really wanted to have sex with me.
Pastor:	How about asking her now for the reassurance you want?
Walter:	Okay . . . uhhh . . . do you want to have sex more often?
Pastor:	Please let me interrupt here. If you are willing, Walt, to practice here in my office, in your own words, I encourage you to ask Tina something specific or descriptive. For example, you could tell her that you want to celebrate your love for each other and then ask if she also wants that with you, on your initiative, perhaps once a week.
Walter:	Do you want to have sex once a week?

Pastor: [interrupting] Yes, Walt, that's more specific. If you are willing, I want to suggest that you add a few words to your invitation such as that you are willing to be the initiator once a week, that you really want to make love with Tina. Are you willing to be bold like that?

Commentary: The pastor notices a distance and a resistance in Walt. Walt is reluctant to even "role play" telling Tina of his desire for her. The pastor encourages him as he shapes and reshapes his invitation to his wife. The pastor is careful not to give orders and instead uses such language as "If you are willing . . ." and "add to." He does not directly confront Walt's hesitancy to approach his wife; the pastor simply supports Walt in becoming more direct with her.

Walter: Sure. Tina, I do love you and do want to have sex with you and I will speak to you about that once a week.

The pastor, with a warm smile, gives an encouraging nod to affirm Walt for making himself vulnerable to Tina.

Tina: I'd like that. [soft-spoken, not much energy shown]

Pastor: What would you need, Tina, to feel more excited about Walt's decision to seek you out at least once a week?

Tina: I don't know. . . . It sounds okay.

Pastor: But . . . ?

Tina: But I don't want to just "have sex." I want something more. [pause]

Pastor: Specifically, what more do you want?

Tina: I'm not sure. I'm willing to . . . uhh . . . uhhh . . . make love. [the last two words in a low, soft, embarrassed voice] It's just that, well, it's how we feel that counts a lot.

Pastor's Silent Reflections: She seems almost afraid to declare that she wants love more than sex. She's still a very reluctant partner in Walt's plan. More protections are needed here.

Pastor: Tina, will you share with me and with Walt what the difference is, for you, between "having sex" and "making love"?

Tina: Uhhh . . . sure. "Having sex" is just doing it. People do it with people they don't even know. "Making love" means not feeling like a sex object; that sex is not the goal, love is.

Pastor: Thank you. Walt, I'd like to hear what you think about the difference between "having sex" and "making love"?

Walter: Well . . . I agree with her.

Pastor: It is good for you two to be clear on that.

Commentary: The pastor probably knows that Walt and Tina are not clear on the definitions of "having sex" and "making love," and yet he wants to reinforce their thinking. He does so with an affirmation or reward that may help strengthen their attitude toward love making.

Pastor: So, then, Walt, when you approach Tina will you make it clear to her that you love her and want to make love with her?

Walter: Yes, I will.

Pastor: And Tina, when Walt approaches you for love making rather than for having sex, will you respond to him with warmth and encouragement?

Tina: Yes. I'd like that. I'm getting excited just thinking about it.

Pastor's Silent Reflections: If I dared, I'd ask them to do a rehearsal for Walt's approach and Tina's response. Is that an intrusion on their privacy? Yes, I think so. They would probably be too embarrassed to practice in front of me. Yet how do I know?

Pastor: Okay. Good for you! I think you have done *great* here today. You have some serious hurt in your marriage. You did not try to take on all your problems at once but did take one important part for consideration this week, that of you, Walt, initiating love making once a week. To increase your power to keep that commitment, you made a distinction between "having sex" and "making love" and you, Walt, agreed to ask Tina to make love with you. You, Tina, agreed to respond to Walt with warmth and encouragement. I believe this is an important step toward celebrating your love in marriage just the way God designed love and sex in the first place. How does it sound to you to set a time now for us to get together, say, two weeks from now, so we can talk about how well you have done and about the next change you want to make in your marriage?

Both: Sure. Thank you.

Two weeks later Tina and Walt were back and ready to talk.

Pastor: So how have you been doing?

Commentary: The pastor begins with an open or "blurred" question so that Tina and Walt can begin anywhere they want. The pastor does not "check up on them" by pressuring them to tell him whether or not they made love each week.

Walter: Well [smile], we kept our bargain . . . and . . . [looks at Tina for approval] she even came on to me once, too.

Pastor: Way to go! I'm proud of you both. How do you feel about yourselves and your marriage now?

Tina: I am more hopeful we can make it. We have a long way to go yet.

Pastor: I understand that. What do you believe might be the next step you could take to develop a finer marriage?

Commentary: The pastor is again inviting focus, specificity, so that today's dialogue will likely be a clear plan for their next step.

Tina: Well . . . I need to know that Walt loves me. I mean I know he loves me but I need to hear it.

Pastor: I understand. I believe that you want Walt to make love with you through words as well as sexually. Is that correct?

Tina: Yes. That's it exactly. I need to hear it.

Pastor: Walt, are you willing to explore ways to make love verbally and then check out with Tina if those are ways she would like?

Walter: Sure. [said with a not very excited speech manner]

Pastor: Good for you. I'd like to share with you for a moment one big difference between men and women, in God's design. Men seem generally to get turned on by what they see and by touch. So some men buy magazines with photos of nude women in them, yet women are not much inclined to buy magazines with pictures of nude men in them. Women usually enjoy touch as much as men. Another big difference is that women usually, when hearing words of love, get much more excited than men do . . . hearing words of love. So Tina might agree to display her body in sexy ways for you, Walt, and you might agree to give her delightful words expressing your love for her. The two sexes are just different; it is not a matter of right or wrong, we are just different.

Walter: Yeah, I know. I can see what you mean.

Pastor: Great! So will you give Tina some words of love now, here?

Walter: Sure. [more energy] I do love you. I'm glad I'm married to you. You're the only woman for me. I think you are sexy and I really want to be with you . . . a lot!

Tina: Thank you. I feel good hearing that. I like to hear those kinds of words from you.

Pastor: Good for both of you. Now that's how you can have more love in your marriage. Walt, as you give love words, and Tina, as you let him know how much you enjoy those words, you will get closer and closer. Of course doing that may not be as easy at home as it was for you here today. There is probably wisdom in looking at how you might block yourselves at home. What might be scary for either of you at home, making love with words like this?

Tina: I enjoyed what he . . . what you, Walt, said to me.

Walter: I know. I am glad to tell you that I love you.

Pastor: Does it make you a little scared to say that?

Walter: Well, some. I mean she may still say "No."

Tina: Well, if the only reason you are telling me that you love me is to get sex, I may not want to!

Pastor: Please let me interrupt. Now I ask you each to slowly ask yourselves what just happened that prompted such strong feelings. [pause] Now if you are willing please give your answers to each other.

Commentary: The pastor interrupted an argument before it became intense. For purposes of understanding Tina and Walt better, he could have let them quarrel for two or three minutes before asking them to let him interrupt. Perhaps the pastor is uncomfortable about the expression of unpleasant emotions and therefore unconsciously blocked the exchange to meet his need. Perhaps he believed that they needed to focus on the positive in order to gain more confidence and hope for themselves. Ideally, the pastor would be consciously aware of his purposes in interrupting at this moment.

Walter: That's just how we get into the mess we're in. No matter what I do, I don't say it right or something and then she flies off the handle.

Pastor: So you have some fear that no matter how much you love Tina with words, she will still be disappointed in you. Is that it?

Walter: You got that right.

Pastor: Okay. Tina, what happened inside you just a moment ago?

Tina: I just felt discouraged, put down, like you were saying what I wanted to hear just to get what you want.

Commentary: Both Tina and Walt are now probably exhibiting evidence of childhood wounds that prompt them to exaggerate their pain with each other now. If the wounds are deep, referral to a full-time counselor will probably be necessary.

Pastor: Tina, will you ask Walt if his words were true, and if so, will he repeat them?

Tina: What? I don't understand.

Commentary: Her confusion is further evidence that Tina is bringing into the present some childhood rejections that make her more sensitive now.

Pastor: Will you ask Walt to declare to you that the words of love he gave you a few moments ago were true?

Tina: Were they?

Pastor: Let me interrupt again. For practice's sake, Tina, will you ask him in descriptive form for what you want?

Commentary: The pastor interrupts when he believes these people are starting to engage in self-defeating behavior. This is a feature of Strategic Pastoral Counseling. In long-term therapy the counselor might let this destructive process run for some time in order to get a more definitive diagnosis and to better interpret to them the nature of their pathology.

Tina: [smiling] Yes. Walt, will you tell me if the words of love you gave me were true or not?

Walter: I meant what I said! I love you. I think you are sexy. I want to be married to you.

Pastor: Walt, inside yourself, what might be making you tense as you say those words?

Commentary: The pastor is alert to incongruence between nonverbal and verbal language. Until there is more congruence these two people are not likely to succeed in their commitments. This was an excellent intervention.

Walter: That she might not, doesn't seem to, believe me.

Pastor: How about asking her if now she believes you?

Walter: Do you believe me now?

Tina: Yes, I do, very much. [she smiles, Walt relaxes, smiles]

Pastor: Good for you. Now I ask you to notice carefully what you have just done. Tina, you asked directly for what you wanted: that Walt tell you whether or not his words of love were true. You also identified that you were fearful of being so bold because maybe he only wanted sex and didn't really love you that much. Then, Walt, you agreed to reaffirm your love for Tina even though you felt apprehensive that she might not believe you or that what you say might not be enough for her. Instead of giving in to your fears you went ahead. Now both of you have a strong basis for being confident in each other's love. The next time you have a need of each other, will you ask for what you want in such positive and descriptive language? Walt, as I understand it you are now prepared to initiate love making with Tina once a week and to make love with her using words of endearment as part of love making. I believe you also will make verbal love with her at other times not related to sexual love making. Are you willing to do that?

Commentary: The pastor summarized well what Walt had said and then added an idea of his own—to make verbal love as well as sexual love.

Walter: Yes. I want to do that.

Pastor: Good for you. And, Tina, I believe you have declared that you want to celebrate your love with Walt in sexual ways and that you will delight him visually at times and let him know that you are excited by his words of love. Are you willing to do that?

Tina: Yes. I'm going to enjoy this. [grinning]

Pastor: All right! You seem to me to be growing in being expressive of your love to each other in just the ways that the other wants to receive love. Suppose we meet again in two weeks to see what other improvements you want to make in your relationship?

Both: Yes. Let's set a time now!

Pastor's Silent Reflections: They both seem much more confident now. I think they can make it. Strange though, these two Christian people have not really drawn upon their faith to gain hope and confidence for what they want to accomplish. I wonder about that. Should I have suggested that? Yes. How come I held back? Maybe

I don't have sexual things and Christian things as closely integrated as I thought.

Two weeks later Walt and Tina arrived. They seemed fairly close and affectionate as they took side by side seats and smiled at each other.

Pastor: Well, you two look rather happy about something.

Walter: We're doing pretty good!

Tina: Yes. We're feeling love.

Pastor: Good for you! I'm sure the Lord is smiling at you both with delight and joy. [pause] How do you want to work to improve your marriage today?

Walter: Well, we've pretty much reached the goal I had when I came in here. And I think Tina feels the same way.

Tina: Yes. We're relating well now. I just hope we don't slip back somehow into the old way.

Pastor: Perhaps now is a good time to build in some strategies for coping with the temptation to slide backward. Do you want to do that here today?

Commentary: The pastor is now moving toward the *Disengagement* stage because this couple seems to have gotten what they need for now. He also asks for a specific focus for this session. He does not encourage them to talk in a wandering, unfocused manner. He has also noted that Walt and Tina did not pick up on his suggestion of spiritual helps for their marriage when he referred to the Lord's joy in their new love.

Both: Sure. How can we do that?

Pastor: Well, I can make some suggestions. You could read a Christian marriage builder book. I could recommend several if you like. A second suggestion is that you both be very clear with yourselves about the roots of your fears of being open verbally with each other about your sexual needs. Walt, I believe you have stated that you sometimes fear that no matter how you tell Tina of your love for her it will never be good enough. And, Tina, I believe you have shared with us that your fear is that Walt does not value you, your being, and is saying only what you want to hear in order to get what he wants: sex.

Tina: But I haven't been feeling that way lately.

Pastor: Good for you. Still, the dark side of all of us never is entirely erased. Paul wrote in Romans something like, "I don't understand myself! The good that I intend to do, I don't. The evil that I intend not to do, I do!" So if Paul continued to wrestle with his dark side all his life, I imagine you will be tempted to slide backward some of the time. That is certainly part of my life—a continuing struggle to be aware of and cope with my dark side.

Tina: I guess so.

Pastor: Well, if either one of you begins to feel that you are sliding backward, one thing you have learned to do here is to ask for what you want in positive language. Walt, what do you need to ask for when you are apprehensive that Tina will not enjoy your words of love?

Walter: I need to ask her if she believes me and if there are other words of love she would like to have from me.

Pastor: Beautiful! Way to go. How about you, Tina?

Tina: I need to ask Walt to tell me that he loves me and that he means what he says or else I will start to feel like a sex object again.

Pastor: I enjoy hearing you both being so clear like that. [pause] I'd like to ask you a question here. I've not heard you tell of making use of your faith as you work to grow and learn how to love each other. Am I hearing you accurately?

Walter: Well, I pray and all, but I never prayed about this.

Tina: It would seem . . . kinda strange to talk to God about sex . . . though [laughs] sex was his idea!

Pastor: It surely was and the Bible teaches that God created sex for humans as a way of celebrating in marriage, sexually, a kind of a sacrament of "oneness," the purpose of Christian marriage. We only make love a few times in a lifetime for the purpose of making babies, but we make love thousands of times for celebrating love. How does that sound to you?

Tina: I never thought of it that way. Sex wasn't talked about much when I was growing up. I don't know that I ever heard it mentioned in church, except maybe our pastor preaching against adultery.

Pastor: So you might pray together to ask God to help you enjoy celebrating your love sexually.

Walter: I think we could.

Tina: Yes. That would be okay.

Pastor: Well, then, how about our having prayer now and asking God to help all three of us to be sexual and loving in just the way God created us? [reaching out to join hands] Dear Lord, our God, we three, Walt and Tina and I, join together in prayer to thank you for creating love and marriage and sex, for helping us celebrate our love in sexual passion and play. We believe you want us to enjoy our bodies and our emotions and to share love through the beautiful words we give to our mates. Please help Tina and Walt to laugh and wrestle and have orgasms and talk of love in ways that fulfill them both, not once a week or twice a week but as often as they like. In Jesus' name we pray, amen.

Commentary: Without telling Walt and Tina what they "should" do, the pastor did invite them to seek spiritual help with what they seem to regard as a very "earthy" need. The pastor made the prayer explicit as a model for Walt and Tina as they pray privately. Over the years ahead they may more thoroughly comprehend the will of God in human sexual love.

Many Christian married couples get into serious conflict because they have not yet learned to understand how the opposite sex thinks, feels, and behaves in matters of sexual love. Often each partner simply assumes that his way or her way is the way the other feels and then feels angry and critical when the partner is different. By helping couples become more aware of gender differences, especially those that show up in sexual behavior, we can help them achieve a happier integration or spiritual oneness in their sexual play.

5

Sexual Difficulties, Past and Present

This chapter will take up sexual difficulties faced at one time or another by most people. Almost everyone has had powerful sexual fantasies, has masturbated, has looked at something pornographic, or has engaged in some level of exhibitionism and voyeurism. In addition, some people are "sex addicts" while others have been or are sexually promiscuous. Married couples usually have some difficulties at times with male sexual dysfunction ("impotence") and generalized inhibited desire ("frigidity"). Also, some people have engaged in premarital sex and feel guilty about that or in some other way have reduced joy in marriage because of premarital experiences.

In helping people deal with sexual difficulties, our task is to bring God's gospel of hope, forgiveness, and understanding as well as his plan for delightful, sensuous, and erotic sexual fulfillment. As we now bring the Good News to bear upon each of these sexual difficulties, we hope you will recall your own sexual difficulties and apply these biblical insights to your own needs. Then, we believe, you will be even better prepared to care for people through pastoral counseling.

Sexual Fantasies

Sexual fantasies may lead to lust but are not the same thing as lust. Lust means to be consumed by or obsessed with sex. If sexual fantasies lead to lust, they are sinful; they involve unloving behavior toward the object of our lust and toward God and ourselves as well. Suppose a man fantasizes regularly about a neighbor by visualizing her in the nude. If he continues these thoughts he will begin to imagine kissing her and then having intercourse with her. He is using her as a sex object and invading her privacy even though she does not know it. His lustful thoughts and feelings may lead to his beginning to flirt with her and then to an affair. His adulterous lust for her may lead to a deeper level of physical adultery with her. His relating to her as a sex object will almost certainly condition him to relate to other women in the same way.

In contrast, if a man fantasizes a few times about an imaginary woman or even a celebrity whom he will never meet, he may enjoy the sexual excitement but not become obsessed. This would not be lust. If he begins to collect pictures of this woman and to write her and to imagine running off to Tahiti with her, that is sinful lust. If this man is making love with his wife and pretends his wife is this celebrity, he is violating his wife and engaging in lust. However, if he is making love with his wife and imagines that they are out on the beach in a secluded place and several beautiful women walk by and smile delightedly at him, and that adds to his sexual excitement with his wife, that is not lust.

A key insight into whether or not something is lustful is to identify the need the person is attempting to meet with these fantasies. The answer may not be as obvious as it first sounds.

For example, if a woman day dreams frequently about being in the arms of a certain man and she asks herself why, she may then answer, "Because he is so strong, virile, and bold with me." She can then ask herself, "In what way is my husband not being strong, virile, and bold with me?" Almost certainly, she will become aware that something has slipped in their marital relationship so that her husband seems more "wimpy" than before. By talking openly with him she will help them both regain the best of their relationship. She might explain, "John, you know, something you used to do a lot was truly pleasurable for me and I've been missing that lately. When you used to pick me up and carry me to the bedroom to make love, that was usually a great turn on. Would you enjoy doing that more?"

John may think a moment and then explain, "I guess when I hurt my back in that fall I took on the ice last winter, I stopped picking you up. I didn't mean to stop forever. I like doing that. As soon as the kids are asleep, I'm coming for you!"

The main aspect we are highlighting here is that sexual fantasies are designed to meet some need. By identifying what the need is we may decide that the fantasy is fine and Christian and then discover a loving way to get the fantasized need met in faithful marital love.

You are taking a long drive on an interstate highway and are getting drowsy and thus becoming a dangerous driver. You start having a sexual fantasy for fun and for alertness! However, if the fantasy is actually a wish for love making with someone other than your spouse and is a mental acting out of resentment toward your spouse, talking out the actual source of the resentment with your spouse would be the Christian and loving thing to do.

Sexual fantasies can be harmless moments in which our bodies and emotions are keyed up in a delightful manner. Sexual fantasies often make available to our conscious minds some unmet emotional or sexual need so that we can take appropriate action to get that need met. However, sexual fantasies can become an end in themselves, can be a rehearsal of adultery or some other sexual sin so that we are more likely to actually do the act. The main key to recognizing the difference between lustful fantasies and delightful fantasies is to discern whether or not the day dreaming adds to the heart-to-heart sharing love and sexual fulfillment of our marital sexual love.

Masturbation

The Bible is replete with warnings about dangerous sexual acts such as sex with parents or extended family (Lev. 18:6–14), same sex people (Rom. 1:24–27), and animals (Lev. 18:22–23). However, there is not one word in the Bible warning us that masturbation is harmful!

An old medical term for masturbation was "onanism" but the sin of Onan was not masturbation. In Genesis 38:8 Onan is presented as the older brother of Er who had died. According to biblical teachings Onan was to marry his brother's childless widow and have a son by her so that in her old age the son could take care of her. This was a form of social security. Onan did not want responsibility for supporting the woman and a baby she might have by him that would not truly be his. He went so far as to have intercourse with her, but he withdrew just before orgasm and spilled his semen upon the ground. His purpose was to avoid having a baby to care for, and by doing this he refused to honor his deceased brother and provide for the widow in her old age. This was not masturbation!

The "verse" quoted to most of us years ago, "It is better to cast your seed in the belly of a whore than to spill it upon the ground," does not occur in Scripture! There is no such verse! There is no word in the Bible against masturbation.

Jesus did warn us that lust can be mental as well as physical. If we masturbate while fantasizing about having intercourse with someone whom we know but to whom we are not married, we are practicing either fornication or adultery. This mental adultery makes physical adultery more likely to happen with that person. It may lead to our feeling consumed by thoughts of this person. Lust is sinful; masturbation is not.

Exhibitionism and Voyeurism

We are all exhibitionistic and voyeuristic to some degree some of the time without this necessarily being sinful. Sometimes our Christian ethics are complicated by the issue of degree of the act, inner motivation for the act, and degree of impact on other persons who may be involved. That is surely true in these behaviors.

We may display our bodies in provocative ways almost anywhere—at the beach or the gym or the office. If what we do violates the privacy of the viewer, if it is compulsive, or if it is contrary to civil law, then we are into sinful exhibitionism. Because this behavior is often so exhilarating it is very difficult to overcome except when it is a relatively normal adolescent acting out over a period of a year or two.

Female exhibitors are usually trying to reassure themselves that they are sexually attractive because they seriously doubt that they are of any value as persons. Male exhibitors are usually trying to shock female viewers. The more startled they are, the more potent these men feel. This is usually related to early boyhood when a boy wanted to "show" his mother that he was different from her.

Males are usually much more intensely aroused by what they see than are females and are thus more likely to engage in voyeuristic behavior. Sometimes this begins accidentally. A pastor I once cared for looked out his office window late one night and saw a couple having intercourse in a car parked behind the church. He became highly aroused and was drawn to that situation on the same night of the week for months afterward. Most adolescents stumble upon some situation such as a girl in the neighborhood who "forgets" to pull the blinds when she is undressing; the boy may stand outside her window for many nights after that.

Voyeurism becomes a serious problem when the perpetrator begins to take more and more invasive action to feed the thrill such as climbing trees or ladders in order to peer in windows, using telescopes, or compulsively hanging out at the bottom of stairways that expose skirted women.

When you have occasion to counsel someone engaging in exhibitionism or voyeurism, a first step is to assess the degree of compulsion and the degree of violation of law involved. If you are working with a frightened teenager who has been caught looking in a girl's bedroom window, you might set up several counseling sessions. One step would be to let him hear your understanding of such behavior. The next step would be a gentle inquiry about any other compulsive sexual behavior he is showing. If there is no other, then you may want to estimate how well the boy is maturing emotionally in most areas of life. If he is doing fairly well, then ask him if he is willing to commit to God and to you to stop peering in this girl's or any other girl's window. If he makes such a commitment, then design a prayer experience with him in which he makes this commitment to God. The next step is to ask him to call you once a week for a month and let you know if he has had a "slip" of any kind. If he has a slip, schedule another appointment. If not, ask him, at the end of the month if he feels ready to stop the weekly calls on the condition that he will call if he has a slip. Affirm him warmly for struggling with strong sexual feelings and responsible godly ways of expressing those emotions.

In contrast, if the person has several sexual compulsions and seems somewhat immature for his or her chronological age, referral to a Christian therapist is probably in order.

Be aware that, as in most things in God's world, a little bit may be delightful and add much to the excitement for living. A little bit more may lead to sinning against God, neighbor, and self. Much more may lead to addictive behavior.

Sexual Addiction

Sexual addiction is now clearly established or recognized as a syndrome that stands alongside addiction to alcohol, drugs, food, or money. Not only do we have Alcoholics Anonymous, Narcotics Anonymous, Overeaters Anonymous, and Debtors Anonymous, there is also Sex and Love Addicts Anonymous (SLAA).

How can sexual behavior become an addiction? To begin understanding the problem we can ask, "What is your favorite defense against emotional pain?" Some people cover hurt with anger. Others cry. Bulemics may make themselves vomit. Others get drunk. Others turn to sexual experience. The common thread relating these all too human behaviors is "self-medication" for pain. When a bulemic induces vomiting, endorphins (forms of a kind of morphine that the body naturally produces) are released. This chemical protects from pain somewhat and may even, at first, trigger a mood of elation. The "high" generated may become addicting.

Sex addicts use sexual contacts to release these endorphins. A man divorced by his wife is in a new apartment and lonely. He leaves and goes to a bar. An hour later he is in bed with a woman whom he has just met. Temporarily he feels elated, and yet usually an hour later he is again depleted and depressed. Two people who are sexually addicted may find each other and use each other, not to make love or to just enjoy sex, but to self-medicate. One of them may begin to slip into depression in the middle of the afternoon and call the other. Together they may masturbate using the phone conversation to get sexually aroused. A man may feel rejected by his wife because she would not make love with him last night; he stops in an adult video room and acts out his rage at his wife and gains a temporary "high" from the sexual activity. The fear of getting caught in some sexually abnormal behavior actually triggers a release of endorphins and helps a person get high. This helps explain why some people become voyeurs when videos and magazines are so easily available. If all a person wanted was to see naked bodies he could purchase some pornography. However, that may not be risky enough for him to attain the high. He goes to the grocery store and "accidentally" bumps up against a woman. Will she slap his face or call the store manager? The risk helps make the act exciting because it releases endorphins.

If someone begins to unburden to you about some sexual acting out, you may begin to think in terms of sexual addiction if the person is describing anonymous sex contacts, sex in which there is no loving relationship, sex that is sought during emotional distress, sex that seems compulsive, and sex that is exciting because it is illegal in some way. This is a very difficult disorder to restrain and there is no "cure" for this or any addiction. You will need to think in terms of both referral to a full-time Christian psychotherapist and to a sex addicts recovery group. Referral does not mean that your pastoral relationship ends; you will still need to have occasional short sessions with this person for prayer and personal support.

A Helpful Pastor's Care

One night after a committee meeting, the pastor was saying goodbye to the few people remaining and was looking forward to making his own exit when Jim asked, "Pastor, do you have a minute?"

Pastor's Silent Reflections: This is going to take more than a minute. Jim seems tense. Slow down. It's okay to be tired and want to leave now. If Jim needs a lot of time think, "reschedule."

Pastor: Sure, Jim, what's up?

Jim: Well . . . uhhh . . . [looking around to see if anyone else is present] I need some help with a small problem. I'm happily married, you know Jean, and this is no big deal, but sometimes when I'm out making a run for work and I drive by an adult video place, I stop and go in. I don't want to but I just go in anyway.

Pastor's Silent Reflections: Jim probably needed a lot of courage to tell me this. This is not all of it. He may be seeing how well I handle this in order to decide whether or not to tell me more. I'd feel better if we were talking in my office but it's 10 P.M. now and I want to get home. I need to encourage him.

Pastor: Thank you, Jim, for trusting me enough to tell me about your pain. I can understand how stimulating those videos can be and how hard it is to avoid them once the excitement is going. Is there something else like that going on with you?

Jim: Well, Jean doesn't know about my going into video places. She would be hurt.

Pastor: Jim, whatever you tell me is in confidence.

Jim: Good. I thought so. Actually, I also buy magazines. . . . I started out with *Playboy* but after a while that was sort of tame and I went on to *Hustler* and now, well, it's about group sex and pretty far out and I've got quite a collection now. I'm afraid. Something's going to happen.

Pastor's Silent Reflections: Jim is probably addicted to pornography. I wonder what makes him vulnerable to that? How good is his relationship with Jean? How good is their sexual relationship? I need to restructure this to be of much more help.

Pastor: Jim, I wonder if we could agree to meet together tomorrow in my office where we could talk more privately and see what options you have about what to do? Could you meet me sometime in the middle of the morning?

Jim: Yeah, I guess so. I'm out all morning and could stop by here about 10:30.

Pastor: Good. I'll look forward to seeing you at 10:30 and we'll just unburden ourselves and perhaps pray together and kind of talk man to man about this problem that troubles most of us men at some time or another.

Pastor's Silent Reflections: I hope that helps him see that I identify with him rather than that I see him as a pervert. Do I see him as a pervert? No, I've looked at some pretty raunchy magazines myself a few times. I liked the feelings that they stirred up. Jim and I are more alike than different. We can walk this walk together.

The next day Jim arrived right on time.

Pastor's Silent Reflections: Jim is motivated, ready. We are entering the *Encounter* stage now. What to do?

Pastor: Well, Jim, how did you feel after you confided in me last night?

Jim: I'm glad I did. I've wondered what you thought of me since I told you.

Pastor: I am encouraged that you told me, pleased that you want to change, not shocked. In my work I've heard it all. In my own life I've done things that were very troubling for me, too. So, I am with you.

Jim: That's a relief—although I can't imagine you doing what I've done.

Pastor's Silent Reflections: We've gained more trust. Maybe he's ready to get to the bottom of this. Be gentle.

Commentary: The pastor is wise not to reveal more of his own sexual acting out as a means of gaining rapport. These two Christians have now made a solid encounter with each other. The pastor is "incarnational" or modeling the truth that Jesus was tempted in every way that we are (Heb. 2:16–18).

Pastor: So, you've done even more? Tell me about it.

Jim: Well . . . I don't know. . . . What makes you think I've done something more?

Pastor's Silent Reflections: Okay. I blew that one. I probably sounded demanding to Jim. I should have asked him if he was ready to tell me about other problems he has. No, I don't need to "should" myself. An apology will just cloud the issue. He sounds guilty about something still hidden. Take it easy.

Pastor: Well, Jim, it's just a hunch. You seem to be hurting a lot and what you told me last night usually leads to deeper hurts. I would like to help you get it all out. So, when you're ready, now or months from now, I'm ready to listen.

Jim: Well, I might as well get it out now.

Jim went on to unburden himself. He was exhibiting himself on a nearby beach and had come very close to being arrested two days before. Thus he decided to begin counseling. The pastor referred him to a Christian with experience in sex therapy and Jim worked through his addiction very well. A key factor here is that the pastor presented himself from the pulpit and in meetings as a man who could understand people and identify with their struggles; he did not present himself as outraged against sin or as a pietist and idealist who would not know much about sin.

Male Sexual Dysfunctions

Men may have difficulty at times with premature ejaculation and with some reduced ability to gain or maintain an erection. There is much debate about how much the source of these problems is psychological and how much is biological. At present there is evidence that premature ejaculation is usually associated with fear of poor performance, fear of closeness, and fear of rejection.

The best evidence now is that most erectile dysfunctions are largely biological in origin. Alcoholism is a major cause. High stress or extenuated illness may drive down testosterone levels and thereby reduce libido or sexual enthusiasm. Many medications, especially heart medications, reduce sexual function somewhat. Long-term and uncontrolled diabetes may also cause erectile problems.

Help is available! A physical exam, possible testosterone injections, self injected penile medications, antidepressant medications, changes in other medications, and stress reduction can often restore full sexual function. Husband-wife dialogue about sexual play, fear of rejection, and the building of trust are usually essential to restore full sexual function.

Premature ejaculation is another problem many men face. Most men do not talk among themselves about such problems and so it is easy to believe that one is part of a very "freaky" minority. The best understood psychological origin of this problem is fear of failure. A man may fear that he will not be able to satisfy his wife, thus "proving" that he is not a man. He may fear that he will ejaculate after only a few thrusts, and his fear will actually trigger the undesired outcome. The man may fear closeness in many ways and quick ejaculation is unconsciously a way to shorten contact and get away to a safe distance.

As we listen to a man suffering with this problem, we may need to offer help for his closeness issues before addressing the premature ejaculation problem. Once he is talking openly with his wife about his feelings, hurts, and hopes, then the so-called squeeze technique can be suggested. They agree to caress each other in early love making until the husband gains an erection. The wife then is to squeeze her husband's penis with her thumb on the underside just below the head of the penis. This will help him pull back from the "point of no return" in ejaculatory control. They can then enjoy each other some more. When the husband is again becoming quite aroused, his wife can squeeze him again. With such repetitions, both husband and wife grow in trust and reduce fear of premature ejaculation. The husband can make entrance and then withdraw and have his wife do the squeeze. He can then reenter and when he begins to feel somewhat aroused, withdraw and ask his wife to do the squeeze again. In relatively little time the man will become more and more aware of his arousal level, more confident of his control, and more able to thrust a while, stop a while, and thrust some more before deliberately ejaculating.

An Example of Hope and Help

Monday morning the pastor was a bit tired from Sunday's ministry and needing some quiet time to organize for the week ahead. At that moment Ruth Jones knocked and asked if she could talk a "few minutes" about "something." The pastor noticed that her eyes were sad, almost teary, and she seemed fearful and hesitant. He invited her in, spoke to his secretary to hold all calls, closed his office door, and asked Ruth to take a seat on the divan. He pulled up a comfortable chair near her.

Pastor: You seem to be hurting about something. I'm glad you stopped by to talk. What seems to be the problem?

Commentary: The pastor gives her two compliments to help her feel encouraged; then he asks a brief question to open up more dialogue. He makes no speech about how much he wants to help. He does not make small talk to "help her relax."

Ruth: Well, uhh, I don't know if you are the person to talk with about this. Oh, I mean, not that you can't help . . . but . . . uhhh . . . I just don't know where to turn. [pause]

Pastor: I want to help.

Commentary: The pastor is brief and clear and does not pressure Ruth to open up.

Ruth: Harry, you know my husband I think, even though he only comes to the worship service. Well, uhhh . . . he would be very upset if he knew I told you this. [pause]

Commentary: The pastor waits, does not rush in with a long reassuring speech. His attentive, relaxed body posture, not looking at his watch, conveys what Ruth needs to know and feel about his readiness to hear her.

Ruth: We are arguing a lot these days about sex. You see, he can't . . . uhhh . . . I mean most of the time the last few months he tries to but he can't, if you know what I mean.

Pastor: Is he having trouble getting and maintaining an erection?

Commentary: By comfortably using the word "erection" and asking the question, the pastor demonstrates his readiness to deal with the issue.

Ruth: Yes! [She sighs, relaxes somewhat, and looks more active.] When he can't do it he blames me. I do all I know to do but it doesn't help. I don't enjoy . . . uhhh . . . sex as much as he does, I suppose, but I like it and want him to enjoy it with me. But I don't think I should be so angrily criticized about it.

Pastor's Silent Reflections: These people are really hurting. He's probably full of fear about his manhood. He may be having an affair that is helping cause this problem. She is blaming herself and he is blaming her. I need to understand, give compassion, build relationship.

> **Pastor:** You sound sad and hurt and yet you also seem to want to help Harry. What else about this is troubling for you?

Commentary: The pastor shows compassion by tuning in to Ruth's feelings and motives and by not asking for facts. He simply invites her to say more.

> **Ruth:** Well, that's it, I guess. I've talked with him about seeing the doctor but he just gets angry. I don't think he would ever agree to come and talk with you; that would be humiliating for him. But I just can't keep on taking this much longer.

> **Pastor:** Enough is enough and you want to start finding help for him and for yourself, is that it?

Commentary: The pastor mirrors his understanding of her feelings and meanings.

> **Ruth:** Yes! What do you think could be the problem?

Pastor's Silent Reflections: Look out! She could use whatever I say to tell her husband that I said he is the problem, not her.

Commentary: She has asked for input from the pastor. He waited until she asked. Now she will likely be more creative in dialoguing with him about possible helps.

> **Pastor:** Well, my understanding is that very often this problem is caused by biological factors such as stress causing testosterone levels to drop. Sometimes an illness causes the same thing. Sometimes it is caused by guilt feelings over something sexual. Sometimes it is an expression of the husband's rage at his wife. Has Harry been under a lot of stress the past six months or so?

Commentary: Ruth stated that the problem started about two months ago and if stress is a major factor it would probably take several months for it to strongly influence testosterone levels.

> **Ruth:** Well, his company has merged with another larger company and there have been lots of changes and I know he is worried that he might lose his job. He has been on the fence about that ever since the merger was announced a year ago.

Pastor: So, that might be a cause. How much is Harry's masculinity connected to his work success?

Commentary: Again the pastor asks a question to invite Ruth to share more. He listens and cares as his primary task. He suppresses his need to give answers or advice.

Ruth: Oh? I hadn't thought about that. Maybe so. I thought he was more worried about it in terms of money, income. He likes his job, has some close men friends there. Before the merger began he usually came home feeling pretty good. He's really hurting now.

Pastor: I can imagine he is worried both about his job and his being unable to enjoy sexual love making with you. Do you think he might be willing to come by with you or have me come by your home to talk about his work and the stress he is feeling?

Ruth: He would probably not object to you dropping by one evening to talk about work stress. But he would be upset if he knew I had told you about his . . . uhhh . . . sex problem.

Pastor: I understand. What you and I have shared here today is confidential on my part. How do you feel about giving me permission to tell him that you mentioned the merger to me and that these were difficult days and would I come by and talk a bit and pray with you?

Commentary: The pastor skillfully develops a clear contract about what he will and will not say about this conversation.

Ruth: Oh, that would be wonderful!

Pastor: Let's see how we could work that out. Tomorrow night I have a committee meeting that starts at 8 P.M. Could I come by and see you for half an hour, say at 7 P.M.?

Commentary: Mentioning the committee meeting helps make clear that this will be a time limited visit. That normally helps people do counseling work more effectively.

Ruth: Yes! Harry usually gets home about a quarter to six. We'll have a light supper and be ready whenever you get there.

Pastor: What would be the most helpful way to let Harry know that I am planning to stop by?

Commentary: The pastor is still working to get a clear contract or understanding of the structure of the visit; this is very important.

> **Ruth:** Well, I don't know. He'll probably wonder what I have told you. If I tell him, he'll probably get angry. You wouldn't just drop by?

Pastor's Silent Reflections: I guess I could do that. Still . . . no, I'm trying to please Ruth. My dropping by would be deceitful and an invasion of Harry's privacy. He would see through that in a minute and that would ruin all chances of help.

> **Pastor:** I could do that. However, I wonder how it would be if I called him at work tomorrow and explain that you had expressed concern about all the work stress he has been having and that I would like to come by and give some support and encouragement?

> **Ruth:** That's good. Okay. I'll look forward to your stopping by.

> **Pastor:** How could we pray together now for you and Harry that would help the most?

Commentary: The pastor offers to pray with Ruth and asks her to think about the kind of prayer that would be the most meaningful to her at this moment. This is more likely to be helpful than if the pastor prays in the mode that would be most helpful to him.

This pastor went on to help Harry become willing to see his physician and obtain medications to reduce stress and depression. After three or four weeks he told the pastor he was "fine again."

Female Sexual Dysfunctions

The kinds of sexual dysfunction described in the previous section and in this one sometimes come up in counseling sessions with couples. Couples will likely be sharing the kinds of emotional problems we describe in the next chapter and then mention these sexual dysfunctions. One reason for this is that many people will turn first to their physicians for help with these problems. There is also the inhibiting problem of the gender of the pastor and the counselee. Men have great difficulty talking about premature ejaculation and erectile difficulties with another man, physician or pastor, and would very rarely mention this to a woman pastor. Women, however, are often more willing to seek help and to talk about their sexual problems, and they may approach a male pastor with these. A

woman pastor may have much more to contribute to women parishioners in this area.

The three dysfunctions women are most likely to bring up are
lack of sexual interest or arousal, pain in intercourse due to lack
of vaginal lubrication or muscle tension, and orgasmic inhibition.

Often wives complain that their husbands want sex much more
than they do. This usually causes conflict. The man feels unloved
because his wife does not seem to enjoy sex with him. The woman
feels unloved because her husband seems to want sex from her
more than a relationship with her. One cause of lack of desire is
fatigue. A woman who works outside the home and who is also a
homemaker and mother has little energy for her husband or for
herself.

A common cause of lack of desire is that the husband does not
make love in ways that are exciting for the wife. He may neglect
foreplay and move too quickly to genital touching and then to
orgasm. He may not whisper words of love early in the sexual
encounter. The wife may be reluctant to teach him ways in which
she enjoys love making and instead may just avoid him. Helping
her feel empowered to talk with her husband about her needs is
as powerful assistance a pastor can give.

The second dysfunction likely to come at times is that the woman
experiences pain on penile entrance. If the husband moves too
quickly to penile entrance for intercourse, the woman may not be
aroused enough to have sufficient lubrication. Penile entrance can
be painful under these circumstances. One tactic is to use a lubricating jelly. A more emotional tactic is to slow down and hug and
kiss and exchange words of love so that the woman has time to
become aroused; then she will lubricate.

There may also be pain for the woman on penile entrance if her
vaginal muscles are very tense. She may be tense because she fears
pain again. She may be tense in these muscles because she is tense
all over, perhaps filled with rage at her husband for neglecting her
or for demanding sex. The key to resolving this problem is communication. The husband needs to work with his wife to resolve
their conflicts so that she is not enraged at him. She needs reassurance that he will not make entrance until her vaginal muscles
are relaxed. For a year or so she may need the reassurance that

lubricating jelly can give her. The pain is an indication of a problem to be solved. Sometimes it is a physical problem that warrants a consultation with her gynecologist. The emotional problem can be solved with loving dialogue and appropriate action.

The third problem involves inhibition of orgasm. This problem may be caused by emotional distress in the husband-wife relationship: by his demand that she have an orgasm; or by his moving too quickly so that she has pain on penile entrance or is simply not aroused enough by the time he reaches climax. It may also be caused by distressful experiences she has had in the past such as negative and harsh sexual education, sexual molestation or rape, or guilt over sexual activity prior to marriage. These relationship issues need to be talked out with emotional release, forgiveness, and new inspiration for sexual fulfillment.

When the woman is emotionally ready to seek orgasmic experience, a kind of reconditioning is usually most helpful. Encourage her to privately explore her own body and pubic area, thanking God for her sexuality and for her sex organs. When she is comfortable at that level, encourage her to put her finger inside her vagina and find her clitoris and again thank God for her sexual organs. When she is comfortable at that level, encourage her to gently stroke her clitoris and to enjoy the sensations of arousal and joy just as God intended when he gave her a clitoris. Suggest that she continue to orgasm if she feels like it or just enjoy touching if that is how she feels. When she is ready, then help her have emotional permission from God to proceed to orgasm and afterward to thank God for this gift from him. The next step is for her to ask her husband to very, very gently caress her clitoris until she reaches orgasm and again to thank God for reaching this goal. The final step, of course, is for relaxing and trusting her body to let herself have an orgasm in penile intercourse some of the time and to feel pleasure in those other experiences in which she does not have orgasm. When she does not have orgasm in penile intercourse, she and her husband can have an understanding that she will want him, some of the time, to caress her clitoris until she does have orgasm. He will likely need help to understand that, unlike most men, she may not want such stimulation every time.

Some individuals will discuss these problems openly with you if you let them know that you are available for such counseling. Others will discuss these problems with their physicians and may want support from you that the help they are receiving is Christian. Some will need referral to a Christian counselor who is very helpful in these sexual matters. These are not merely medical problems for which we have little to contribute. These are partly emotional and relational problems in that area the Good News has much to contribute!

Sexual Inhibition

One source of sexual inhibition is argumentativeness. By attacking each other when sexual needs are not met or for other reasons, sexual responsiveness is even further diminished. Some couples need to grow in conflict resolution skills so they can reduce their anger at each other. Pastors have much to offer about "being angry but not sinning" (Eph. 4:26) and about "turning the other cheek" (Matt. 5:39). As couples learn these skills they can then grow in trust, which will enable them to be more and more sexually playful and open with each other.

Sexual shyness or uptightness also inhibits the sexual joy God intends for us. Perhaps one partner wants to try different positions, incense, music, or lights; the other wants to have sex only in the dark. One partner reluctantly agrees to sex provided it is done in the same routine way on the same day of the week; the other may push for variety. One person is available for sex but usually is very bored; the other is hurt by the boredom of the partner. One person does not have orgasm and the other feels inadequate and rejected by this "lack of response."

These couples need to grow in sexual spontaneity and playfulness. They need pastoral reassurance that God intends for us to play sexually and to experiment with different sexual positions, methods, and moods within marriage. The more people understand that sexuality is primarily for love making and secondarily for baby making, the more uninhibited they may become.

Most of these sexual problems are actually relationship problems. Once couples are heart to heart with each other they will be empowered to be sexual with each other in Christian love, joy, and passion.

Conclusion

There are many sexual difficulties in most marriages. Much spiritual maturity is required for "the two to become one." Fortunately the sexual difficulties are relatively easy to correct— once the relationship issues are well managed in love, forgiveness, and trust.

References

Joyce J. Penner and Clifford L. Penner. 1990. *Counseling for sexual disorders: Resources for Christian counseling.* Dallas: Word.

Clifford Penner and Joyce Penner. 1981. *The Gift of Sex: A Christian guide to sexual fulfillment.* Waco: Word.

6

Sexual Disharmony Revealing Relationship Disharmony

$\mathbf{M}$any couples will describe their marital problems in terms of sexual complaints when actually their difficulty arises from a basic dysfunction in their relationship. When these people learn how to relate in love and open communication, they may find it relatively easy to solve their sexual problems. However, if they focus narrowly on their sexual problem and do not address the deeper relationship problem, they may not benefit much from pastoral counseling.

The following examples of Strategic Pastoral Counseling illustrate common marital relationship problems that are often presented as sexual problems.

Fear of Closeness

A pastor was approached by a woman in his congregation who wanted to "stop by for a few minutes to talk about something." After they were seated comfortably and made some emotional contact with each other, the woman began.

Doris: My husband and I never argue much and I suppose I should be quite happy—but there's something wrong. I sense some kind of a pattern but I can't quite seem to put my finger on it.

Pastor: What do you see so far?

Doris: Well, we get along okay but there's no romance or fun. Somehow we always seem to have a problem and that keeps us apart.

Pastor: If you're willing, please share a recent specific example.

Doris: Maybe it'll help if I describe what happened Friday night. We went out to dinner, held hands at the movie, and generally had a good time. On our way home I started feeling tense. My husband, Rick, said, "You're awfully quiet." I just said, "I'm relaxed, feel good, enjoyed tonight." He kind of paused and in a discouraged sounding voice said, "Me too." I asked him, "Is something the matter?" He seemed a bit more tense and said, "No! I'm just looking forward to getting home with you . . . time to . . . get it on together. [Doris looks at pastor hesitantly.] Sometimes when I think we have a great romantic mood going, we just seem to ruin it somehow." I told him, "Well, I'd enjoy making love tonight, so don't bring up the past." Rick then got irritated. "Who's bringing up the past!" We said a few more things like that and by the time we got home we had nothing but silence—and no love making. He blames me but we never talk about it.

Pastor: And you see a pattern in this?

Commentary: The pastor is patiently waiting for Doris to see the pattern for herself, which will be more powerful than if he intellectually describes it for her.

Doris: Sort of. I just get a weird feeling of "Oh, oh, here we go again! I know how *this* conversation is going to end." It's like once we start it, we can't stop it, and it always ends the same way.

Pastor: How does it end?

Doris: We aren't speaking and then the next day we act as if nothing happened. He won't talk about it then.

Pastor: And?

Doris: No sex.

Pastor's Silent Reflections: I don't know what is going on here except that for some reason these people avoid sex a lot. She's slightly embarrassed to be telling me this, but seems to be getting more comfortable. Keep on asking her questions! Listen for this "pattern."

Pastor: So, if you hadn't argued the other night, what would have happened?

Doris: We would have continued to enjoy each other, probably have made love, had a nice and lovely evening.

Pastor: Probably?

Doris: Well, I guess . . . I don't know.

Pastor's Silent Reflections: Impasse. I've asked her so many questions I'm afraid she'll feel as if I am grilling her. I don't want to change the subject just because I am unsure about how to proceed. I'll stay with the theme. I'll see what happens if I come at it from a different angle.

Pastor: Suppose your kids were at their grandparents for the weekend and you were catching up on Saturday with homemaking, car maintenance, and that sort of thing and late in the afternoon he subtly suggested that you stop and make love. What would happen?

Doris: We'd do it. No big deal. It would just happen and be kind of over with quickly. No problem.

Pastor's Silent Reflections: If it's not a high expectancy romantic evening they can have sex in a routine way, but if it's a big deal they both may fear closeness; they fear going for something wonderful. That may be the "pattern." I think a summary may help.

Pastor: I'd like to summarize what I think I hear you describing and just ask you to reflect on this and then fill in any gaps you see. Okay?

Doris: That would be fine.

Pastor: What I hear is that if you have a romantic evening that would logically end with some delightful love making, you get irritated with each other over something relatively unimportant and that ruins the romance. On the other hand, if you have an ordinary opportunity to make love, you can do it without much in the way of high expectations or much talking about it. How do you hear that?

Doris: That sounds pretty accurate. I had not seen the pattern that clearly before. It is almost as if we are afraid to . . . get our hopes up about something wonderful. That's sad.

Pastor's Silent Reflections: Progress! They're afraid of closeness, afraid of slow and gentle sexual play, and they seem to be conflict avoiders—they never talk about the problem the next day. What am I feeling toward Doris now? I feel sad with her that they are missing out on so much. I'm feeling some sexiness myself. I still get a little turned on hearing about other people's sex lives. I can remember when Sharon and I have done the same thing as Doris and her husband. Got to be careful and not try to solve my problem through pushing my solution onto Doris. I think the best way to manage my own feelings and to help them is to get Rick involved here.

Pastor: Do you think Rick would be willing to come in with you and talk with me like this?

Doris: Probably. He's rather sensitive though. I guess he'd come in.

Pastor's Silent Reflections: Sounds like Rick will be very reluctant . . . or she *wants* him to be very reluctant. How can I increase the odds? She may be afraid to bring it up to him. I could, might even do it better!

Pastor: Could I possibly call him, ask him to come by alone; and could I have your permission to tell him that we've talked? I will keep confidential all you have shared with me today.

Doris: That's a good idea! And it's okay with me to tell him everything I've told you. I'll try to tell him myself.

The pastor called Rick and he agreed to come by. The pastor felt that for Rick it was less embarrassing to come in than to disagree with his pastor. Three days later they met. After a few minutes of general church comments that Rick used to help himself become more comfortable, the pastor asked Rick to summarize things briefly and Rick described the situation in about the same way Doris had in her session. The pastor suggested that the next meeting involve the three of them. Rick agreed and a date was set for a week later, subject to checking with Doris. In the three-way talk the pastor asked many questions about the childhood background of Rick and Doris in hopes of uncovering the origins of their fears of closeness. Rick recognized that as a boy his mother always favored his older brother, and his father was gone a lot. He learned to play alone. Doris also learned to expect rejection. Her parents expected perfection; if she got three A's and one B, they would comment negatively on the B. With considerable embarrassment she also stated that they made her feel awkward about her body. She was too chubby or too revealing, and body odors were talked about a lot as very disgusting.

Pastor's Silent Reflections: So they've uncovered a lot of the sources of their fear of closeness and the difficulties in trying to enjoy sexual love. I need somehow to give them powerful permission to disobey the parental messages in their heads. First Corinthians 13. But don't preach the answer. Invite them to apply the principle!

Pastor: Thank you very much for letting me share in your discovery of the roots of the problem. Now I'd like to suggest a principle that you might find very powerful for use in solving the problem. First Corinthians 13, the "love chapter," concludes with something like, "When I was a child I thought like a child, I felt like a child, I talked like a child, but when I became a man I put away childish things." We all need to "put away" some things we learned in childhood because as children we all learned some faulty ways of relating. I'm not suggesting that you blame your parents; only that you replace their teachings about fears of rejection in closeness with your own adult beliefs that love is "patient and kind, celebrates what is beautiful."

Doris: I'd like to do that . . . but how?

Pastor: A way to do that is to "do the thing you fear." Doris, my suggestion is that you contribute to a breakthrough for you and Rick by agreeing not to take a shower before your next love making and wear the nightie Rick thinks is your sexiest.

Doris: I . . . uhh . . . really have never liked those things . . . don't have any now.

Pastor: Then let Rick buy one for you and wear it no matter what the "parents in your head argue." Is that a possibility?

Doris: I guess so. [looks at Rick]

Pastor: And Rick, will you then buy a lovely and sexy nightie for Doris? And, if anything is less than perfect in this love making, will you just ignore it and concentrate on having fun? For example, if she's not lubricated when you want to enter, just play some more, okay?

Commentary: The pastor is now inviting these two Christians to use their faith to help themselves enact a heartfelt commitment to change. The pastor is not changing them. They may now choose to live out their faith right there in the room by deciding to change themselves. The pastor has also become quite directive in this counseling, an approach that is quite appropriate for Strategic Pastoral Counseling. His reference to vaginal lubrication was a kind of permission for them to talk with him and each other about such private issues.

Rick: Uhhh, sure, okay. [grinning]

Pastor: And, Doris, will you agree not to reject Rick in any way and not try to be perfect for him at all?

Doris: I agree. This feels like wedding vows or something! [grinning]

Pastor: Good. I hope so! Now, to help empower you both to carry forward these commitments, I wonder if it would be okay if we have prayer and together make these commitments to God?

Both: Sure.

Pastor: Rick, will you tell God your commitments and then ask God to help you keep them?

Rick: I guess so. Yes. I will.

Pastor: Doris, will you do the same?

Doris: Yes, I want to do that.

Commentary: The pastor has now led Rick and Doris to repeat their commitments several times and to dedicate those commitments to God. This may greatly empower them to succeed.

Pastor: I'll close when you are finished with your prayers. Let's join hands as we two or three gather together in Jesus' name, knowing he is now present with us.

[Rick and Doris pray short prayers, reaffirming their commitments.]

Pastor: Dear heavenly Father, the three of us thank you for sexual love and marriage and for bodies that thrill to the very touch of our marriage partners. We thank you that you created that first husband and wife, Adam and Eve, to be naked and uninhibited, making love with laughter and passion. We thank you for the wetness and odors and groans and sighs of sexual love and orgasm. We ask you now to bless the commitments of Rick and Doris that they may be empowered by your Holy Spirit to put away painful childhood fears that they will be rejected if they get close and instead to live in love and sexual passion and play together. In Jesus' name we pray amen.

Two weeks later, Rick and Doris arrived for their next session. Both were grinning, holding hands. Almost as soon as the pastor closed his office door, Doris laughingly burst forth.

Doris: We broke one commitment! I did take a shower beforehand . . . with Rick!

Pastor: Wonderful! I'm sure God had a big smile for both of you at that moment.

Rick: We had fun. No rejection. And, we've gotten together three more times since then!

Doris: We're happy. Rick's happy. I'm happy. Thank you so much. We had no idea you could help us so much . . . Oh! I mean, that you would have training for such intimate . . . oh!

Pastor: Doris, you don't have to be perfect for me either! Thank you both for telling me that you appreciate my being with you in this. Do you each want to reaffirm that you will keep these commitments to put away childish things and to not getting alarmed if you have an infrequent slip back a little?

They both gladly agreed and the three had a thanksgiving prayer.

These two people may discover that their fear of closeness comes out in other parts of their relationships such as in fear of verbally telling their children how much they love them. They may yet need referral if they cannot persist in their new freedom and closeness. Yet if they keep on practicing being aware of those childhood patterns that do not work in adulthood and then "putting away" those patterns by prayerful commitment and then by doing the thing they fear, Rick and Doris may grow all the rest of their lives in freedom to be close.

Self-Centeredness Expressed in Sexual Dysfunction

Laurie had called for a formal appointment, stating that the pastor had married her and Tom seven years before and that now they were headed for divorce. She hoped he could "do something."

Laurie and Tom arrived ten minutes late, dropped into two chairs opposite each other and, without any prompting began.

Tom: She wanted to talk with you, Pastor! I don't think talking is going to help much. She just doesn't understand men, me. She's critical, cold. I love her but there's got to be more to life than talking and complaining.

Laurie: [slightly teary-eyed already] Can you help us? I'm exhausted. We've got two children now. They're four and six and I'm very busy taking care of them and then I'm office manager for Tom's practice. He works long hours and we earn a fine living, but . . .

Tom: That's it. *But.* You're never satisfied. Look at all you have! And you never show any appreciation. We never have any fun!

Laurie: By "fun" you mean sex!

Tom: Well, what's wrong with that! We're married. A man works all day and comes home and wants some appreciation, especially a little lovin' instead of complaining and "being too tired."

Pastor's Silent Reflections: Whew! Too fast! I want to slow them down. Speak slowly. Summarize. Maybe that will help.

Pastor: If I understand what you want Tom, in order to make your marriage better is less criticism and more praise from Laurie, and more sexy play; is that it?

Tom: Yeah! I'm glad *you* understand! Please help Laurie. I'll do anything to help her get her priorities straight.

Pastor's Silent Reflections: So Tom wants what he wants, gets angry when he doesn't get it, believes the problem is all Laurie's, and has little interest in trying to understand her. Narcissistic?

Pastor: I'm encouraged to hear that you will work to help Laurie understand. Laurie, what do you need more of for your marriage to be more fulfilling for you?

Laurie: I don't know exactly. I need for our relationship to be better, you know?

Pastor's Silent Reflections: Must be difficult for Tom to understand such abstractions as "better relationship" when he needs a specific as "sex three times a week and no criticism." I need to ask Laurie to describe in specific, behavioral terms what she wants, to "speak Tom's language."

Pastor: By "relationship" do you mean talking, sharing, opening up feelings, meanings, and motives to each other?

Laurie: Yes! That's it exactly. I *knew* you could help us!

Pastor's Silent Reflections: Watch out for Laurie's praise. She feels understood, which she doesn't get from Tom. She also wants me on her side against him. Neither of them tunes in to the other's viewpoint. Maybe now they will give that a try.

Commentary: Early in the first session the pastor is wisely focusing not on "the problem" but on being sensitive to his relationship with Laurie and Tom. Love is what heals brokenness, not logical solutions or counseling techniques.

Pastor: Are you willing to do some "practice" relating here, now?

Tom: Sure.

Laurie: I guess so.

Commentary: The pastor is now inviting Tom and Laurie to move into new behaviors in the protective environment of his office and personal presence. They are much more likely to do well here than if they attempt this next step at home. If they practice fairly well, that will be an indication that the relationship building was effective. If they agree to practice relating but move toward arguing, the pastor will need to go back to improving his relationship with them.

Pastor: Good for you! So Laurie, what is an area of your marriage you'd like to discuss with Tom now?

Laurie: I don't know. There is so much.

Tom: What about the new car I bought you?

Laurie: I told you I liked it. Thanks.

Tom: Well?

Laurie: Well what? You mean I should go home and jump into bed with you! I'd feel like a prostitute!

Pastor: Tom, if you are willing, I invite you now to look at this from Laurie's point of view. Show her what you understand about how she could feel like a prostitute. Will you?

Tom   [looking at and talking to the pastor, not Laurie] Sure! She thinks she would be giving sex to get a car. But I got her the car because I wanted her to have a good, reliable, car, and . . .

Pastor: [interrupting] And how might that make her feel?

Tom: I don't know, angry, I guess, but I didn't get her the car to get her to give me sex! It's that if she appreciates all I do for her, surely she would want to show me her love by making love more than once every three or four weeks!

Pastor's Silent Reflections: We are getting nowhere. He isn't tuned in to her feelings at all. He only talks about himself. I'm beginning to dislike him. Does he remind me of some of my own narcissism maybe? Slow down. Remember, "You cannot change anyone on the face of this earth but yourself!"

The pastor then worked with Tom and Laurie to set a date for a second session.

Laurie showed up for the session but Tom had his secretary call and explain that he had a last-minute conflict.

Pastor: How have you been relating since two weeks ago?

Laurie: The same. [sighs] We just can't seem to get anything going. All he does is talk about how bad our sex life is. But we . . . uhhhh . . . got together several times since we saw you and he's not any happier.

Pastor's Silent Reflections: Tom probably contrived, perhaps unconsciously, to have a conflicting appointment. He didn't want to be here. He wants Laurie to be the one who needs help, not himself. Laurie seems to want to grow, and yet I have this feeling of discouragement about her, too. Can this marriage be saved? Right now I think they are both too self-centered to be able to be married to anyone. They are going to need weekly psychotherapy sessions for a year or two. I need to make a referral.

Pastor: Laurie, how about considering a different way to get some growing going then? [Laurie nods] I have a friend who is a licensed marriage and family therapist, a fine Christian, who has both the time and the training to give you the help you clearly need. What I'd like is for you to give me permission to call her and summarize what we've uncovered here in these two sessions and then have the two of you call and make an appointment. After you two have seen her for two to three sessions, then I'd like to see you both here together to kind of reevaluate. Are you willing to do that?

Laurie: If you think that's best. [looks sad, slightly scared, perhaps feeling rejected]

Pastor: I can imagine that seeing a therapist is a bit scary and yet she is a kind Christian person and she knows she can't make you do anything. She can help you change yourselves, though. Perhaps you will feel encouraged if I summarize what I think is happening in your relationship with Tom. My understanding is that he works long hours partly because he is "top dog" there and when he comes home he wants to continue to be "top dog." You are to be rested, have the kids out of the way, and be ready to give him your undivided attention whenever he wants it. He wants you to praise him, even adore him, and to show that by exuberant sex. On your side, as I understand the situation, you seem to want him to appreciate you inwardly, to value you for who you are, not just for what you do in bed or at the office or with the children. If you get more assertive about your needs, he may blow up, have an affair, or something else foolish.

Pastor's Silent Reflections: I'll be in trouble if she quotes me to him on that! I'm showing off how discerning I am compared with Tom! Take it easy!

Pastor: The problem doesn't seem to be so much about sex; it's more that Tom may not know how to relate to you inwardly, and you may need to grow some to know how to be both powerful *and* alluring. To learn these kinds of skills you'll both need to be in counseling for some time. I am confident that both of you can learn and can have joy and sexual love together. Go for it!

Laurie: You seem to think we've both got big problems, not just me.

Pastor: Yes. I do.

Laurie: He doesn't think he needs to change.

Pastor: What about Tom would make it difficult for him to admit that he needs to grow?

Laurie: I don't know. [pause] He'd be embarrassed, I guess.

Pastor's Silent Reflections: Right on! But, don't say so to her. If she quoted you to him, he'd probably retaliate by not seeing Dr. Rogers. How many times have I heard this story? Men give love to get sex; women give sex to get love. He's very narcissistic—low empathy, feels entitled to what he wants now! Angry, shame-based. She's self-centered also but in a dependent sort of way. How might I preach on love and empathy to help couples like Laurie and Tom? Jesus and the woman at the well in Samaria? When he *understood* her, she felt enthused and empowered to go and relate to the townpeople who had scorned her. Ooops! Back to Laurie.

Pastor: You may be right. So you are ready to call Dr. Rogers and have given me permission to call her also. If Tom refuses to go, will you go by yourself anyway?

Laurie: I guess so.

Pastor: Good for you. I believe strongly that you will be glad you are taking this step. I'll see you both here after you have seen Dr. Rogers two or three times. God bless you, Laurie. God surely created marriage for love and joy and sexual pleasure, and my prayer now is that you and Tom will feel the powerful love of God helping you both change, not each other, but yourselves over the months ahead.

Commentary: This pastor recognized serious character deficiencies in these two people and knew they would probably need at least several years of psychotherapy to overcome these handicaps. He engaged in the "ministry of referral." As he worked with Laurie and Tom he carefully monitored his own inner reactions to them and recognized several times when he was getting into his own personal needs rather than focusing on theirs. His awareness helped him refocus and turn back to them. Therefore, his mistakes were not damaging and his work did lead to a constructive outcome.

The Sex Object

A frequent problem many couples experience seems to develop when the wife feels like a "sex object" and the husband feels increasingly that she is "not interested in sex." One such couple reported how their problem evolved. They had been married five years and had two small children. This was a first marriage for both. Each had worked prior to marriage and the wife had worked until their first baby was born. Both agreed he was romantic, thoughtful, and very attentive to her during their courtship and the first year of marriage. However, she reported that when the baby was born it seemed to her that suddenly he changed. More and more he treated her like a "sex object.

Pastor: How about telling me what Skip does that makes you feel like a "sex object?"

Candy: He never helps out around the house. He plays with the kids when it suits him but doesn't help me take care of them when I need him to help daily with things like bathing and dressing them. The only time he ever touches me is when he . . . uhhh . . . wants sex. So the way I feel is that all he wants from me is sex.

Pastor: Skip, if you're ready, how about telling me how you see the situation?

Commentary: The pastor is asking questions, inviting dialogue, not doing an intellectual search for answers. As Skip and Candy answer his questions in the presence of each other, they will grow in self-understanding and in similar knowledge of each other. This kind of understanding is much more important than any "answer" the pastor could ever give them.

Skip: What's it get me to be thoughtful? She just doesn't like sex, I guess. Once every week or two and that's all she wants. She's very tuned in to what the babies want, not what I want. She was hot to trot at first, if you know what I mean, but not now. I want to be a liberated husband of the nineties but I need a modern woman to make that work!

Pastor's Silent Reflections: We've made an opening at the Encounter stage. I've known Skip and Candy for five years. They do not seem to be embarrassed to be talking with me about their sexual feelings. I think they are ready to explore those emotions more deeply.

Pastor: Thank you for telling me about your feelings. Now, to help me understand more about the struggle you face, Skip, how about describing for me the problem, not as you see it but as Candy sees it?

Commentary: This strategy first helps the pastor assess just how understanding and compassionate Skip is. If Skip does reasonably well, that will be reassuring to Candy and she will become more trusting of him.

Skip: Oh, I don't know. She's angry that I don't help out around the house, but I work all day and then I come home and mow the grass, maintain the cars, and repair things. She has a lot to do, but so do I!

Pastor's Silent Reflections: He's more defensive, probably knows he doesn't understand Candy's needs very well. He didn't answer my question. I don't think he is ready for me to push him on his understanding of Candy.

Pastor: Thank you, Skip. Now Candy, how about describing the problem from Skip's point of view as you understand it?

Candy: He resents all the time and energy I give the kids and doesn't understand how exhausted I am all the time. It's like he's in competition with the kids to get all he can of my time and energy. I feel like everybody's taking from me and nobody is giving to me!

Pastor's Silent Reflections: They are taking an adversarial stance toward each other, unconsciously wanting me to be a judge who will rule on who is right and who is wrong. As a man I readily identify with Skip. He is young. His sex drive is strong. He feels tricked, that Candy got kids from him and now doesn't value him as much because she is fulfilled in motherhood. Wow! That brings back memories! Jill and I went through the same pattern when our kids were small. I'll need to be careful here and not overidentify with Skip. What about Candy? She probably is much more fulfilled now that she is a mother. It is all new to her. The kids need her so much. A woman's sex drive is often not so orgasmically urgent as a man's and instead she's probably experiencing a deep hunger for closeness with Skip. What to do? Refer? Do a consult? Worth a try.

Between sessions the pastor called a marriage and family therapist in private practice, a church-going Christian, to whom he had made two previous referrals. After a half-hour on the phone in consultation, the pastor gained these insights:

1. Many women's values probably shift when they become mothers; nurturing new life now becomes their strongest godly fulfillment.
2. Skip is sexually frustrated and jealous of his own kids and also feels guilty for feeling that way.
3. Skip and Candy are in an "I win, you lose" attitude and have little empathy for each other for fear that understanding the other person might lead to an "I lose, you win" attitude in themselves.
4. What might help would be to invite them to generate options for a "we-win" outcome, a think-tank brainstorm approach. They could write down on paper some specific changes they could make that would help both of them. I could ask Skip to list what he truly wants to do with and for the kids. Would he enjoy taking care of the home and kids while Candy had all Saturday afternoon off to play, go shopping with a friend, or do anything else she wanted? I could ask Candy how she might regain her energy for playing with Skip. On a week night would she swap child care with another couple so that she and Skip could be at home alone together? Would she then use a paid baby sitter for a "date" on Saturday night? Would she start planning now for a one-week vacation for just the two of them, asking the grandparents to give child care for that time? Would she use the time saved by Skip helping out more with the kids to shower, rest, and gain energy for being with him once the kids are down for the night?

The marriage counselor also suggested that when the written list was developed, the pastor would be wise to ask both of them to reaffirm that they intend to live by their written commitments and to add to it as they grow in "we-win" thinking.

When Candy and Skip came for their next appointment, the pastor began by asking how they were doing and what they wanted to accomplish in this session. They replied that they were talking to each other more but that there was still something that kept them unhappy. The pastor believed that they were ready to get more specific, so he suggested that they write down actual changes each was willing to make in himself or herself. Neither was to suggest changes for the other person. Only changes that were "we-win" were put on the list. After they had a workable list the pastor wanted to help them put the list in a Christian perspective to add depth to their commitments.

Pastor: As you look at your commitments, what is the main spiritual issue here as you both see it now?

Skip: That we love one another the way God intended.

Candy: Yes. It's got to do with love. I'm not quite clear though. I've always known Skip loved me but something was missing—something even more important than the things he has agreed to here today.

Pastor: There are several biblical ideas that might help you interpret what you are feeling. Just listen to your heart for a few minutes as I summarize a bit. The Bible speaks of *agapē* love, a rational, deliberate caring for someone's welfare. In *agapē* we can love our enemies even though we don't like them. The Bible has another word, *philia,* which means "friendship," liking, emotional delight, heart-to-heart sharing.

Candy: *That's* the missing ingredient!

Skip: Yeah. We were friends when we first got married. Lately we've just been work partners who didn't like each other very much. [Skip moves toward Candy, hugs her, glances at the pastor who motions to Skip, "I'll be in the outer office" and quietly leaves.]

By the time the pastor spoke to his secretary about a phone message and returned, Skip and Candy were opening the office door, grinning. The pastor reentered his office and sat with them.

Pastor: You look like friends again! I'm proud of you both! What did you do?

Commentary: The pastor affirms them: "I'm proud of you." He takes no credit for what they've accomplished and instead invites them to celebrate and firm up their work by use of the question, "What did you do?" The more they tell each other, the pastor, and God about the changes they will make, the more likely they will be to make those changes.

Skip: We just realized how much we loved each other and that other couples probably have this same problem and solve it; we can too!

Pastor: How do you feel about your written commitments for making more time for each other?

Skip: I'm ready!

Candy: So am I. With a little more rest, I'll feel, as Skip puts it, "hot to trot" again! He'll see!

Pastor: So you each have your list of written commitments of friendship love to keep. One other suggestion. Here is a brochure that describes Marriage Encounter. The program is lay-led, very inexpensive, is done on weekends, and is designed to help couples continue to build the friendship in their marriage. Jill and I have taken part and benefited from "making encounter" very much. I recommend that you contact the coordinator and see when the next Encounter Weekend is scheduled.

Commentary: The mention of Marriage Encounter is a form of referral. The pastor here is probably working too hard to help. He has brought in a new idea when Skip and Candy are already excited about their plans. This is not a serious error and yet the timing would have been better if the pastor had sent them a pastoral note of prayer and encouragement several weeks later with the Marriage Encounter brochure enclosed.

Pastor: Will you please call me if you start letting your friendship love slip backward? Then I'd like to join with you in prayer now to ask God's blessings on your friendship love and your sexual love and to thank him for helping both of you let go of sex object ways of relating.

Dear Heavenly Father, who created love and marriage and sexual delight, we join together to ask your special blessings upon the marital friendship of Skip and Candy as well as upon Jill and myself. Please, Father, help each of us to share our inward feelings, meanings, and motives as well as to share our bodies and erotic passions. Help us to know the biblical oneness of marriage so that we will delight in each other daily in many ways. And, Lord, please give Candy and Skip an extra measure of commitment to be faithful to the plans they have made and put in writing here today for adding much to the friendship and love of their marriage. In Jesus' name, we pray, amen.

Commentary: In this prayer the pastor identifies with the couple by including in the prayer himself and his wife. He marks out clearly that sexual-erotic passion is part of God's plan for marriage and affirms that heart-to-heart sharing is an essential of godly marriage. He also holds up in prayer the commitments Candy and Skip have made for deepening their joy. This will help them feel truly dedicated to making the plan work.

All the problems this couple face are *not* now solved. However, both are now likely to work on the problems together rather than as adversaries. They may need an occasional follow-up session but may make it without referral to a full-time marriage counselor.

Anger Blocking Sexual Joy

Another example of relationship problems expressed as sexual problems was presented to a pastor by an attractive and successful Christian married couple in his church. Marshall was a handsome and highly effective businessman and lay church leader. He was admired by many but had few close friends. The pastor assumed that when Marshall called to set a time to come by for a talk, he would be presenting a requested plan for church development. However, when Marshall arrived at the church he had his wife Lindsey with him. She looked stunningly attractive as usual and yet her face expressed tension and fatigue.

Pastor: Lindsey, Marshall, come in, have a seat. I'm happy to see you both. How are you doing?

Marshall: Not too well, pastor. That's why we are here. This is a bit embarrassing but something has to be done. Our marriage is in serious trouble. I cannot seem to convince Lindsey how important she is to me and how much she fits into my life. I work long hours, need to be out of town a lot on business, and my work, as you know, Pastor, requires a lot of creative dealing with people. So, when I come home I just want to relax, read, listen to some music, and yet, make love with my wife like most other husbands. That seems pretty normal, doesn't it?

Pastor's Silent Reflections: Marshall sounds logical, makes sense. All I know is that in my heart right now, I don't like him. That is strange. I'm missing something. I'll see what Lindsey has to say.

Commentary: The pastor intuits that Marshall is a controlling person who has taken charge of this counseling session. The pastor then thinks that he would do well to listen carefully so he can at some point comprehend the meaning of his discomfort with Marshall's apparently logical presentation of the problem.

Pastor: Lindsey, how would you describe the situation?

Lindsey   Well . . . uhhhhh . . . [looking at Marshall questioningly] Marshall does work very hard and when he comes home he is entitled to some peace and quiet. I manage the home and children very well so there is little for him to do at home. I think he has lots of time to relax.

Pastor: And what changes would help you enjoy your marriage more, Lindsey?

Lindsey: Oh, I don't know. I guess I need more time to be with Marshall, you know, just to talk and feel close.

Marshall: "Feel close." That's what I want, too, but you're always too tired or out at a meeting of some kind!

Lindsey: I know. I've got to do better. I want you to be happy.

Pastor's Silent Reflections: **Marshall talks as if feeling close and making love are the same thing. Lindsey surprises me here. In church committee meetings she is almost always the chair or the leader. Now she seems to almost surrender to Marshall and yet he is saying that she does not give him enough of herself. There must be some problem beneath what they are describing just now.**

Pastor: Marshall, if you are willing, it would help me if you would tell me how this problem usually comes up at home.

Marshall: Well, like I said, I come home, looking forward to some peace and quiet. The kids are well behaved; they're no problem. Lindsey doesn't yell at me like some wives do. It's just that when I want to go out to dinner and relax without the kids and then come home and sort of end our date by making love, something always seems to go wrong. Sometimes she says it hurts. Other times she says it's no fun for her . . . doesn't climax, and she sort of cries. I ask her what's wrong and she says she doesn't know and by that time I just say to myself, "What's the use?" The mood is broken so I get up and go watch television or something else. I really hope you can suggest some help for her, pastor.

Pastor's Silent Reflections: **Marshall has now made Lindsey the "identified patient." He expects me to "fix" her. I can now understand my negative reaction to him a few minutes ago. He is very controlling. He wants her when he wants her and he wants her out of his space at any other time. If I'm not careful, I will start to try to convince him he is as much to blame as she is. That would simply drive him out of here. Listen! Ask questions. Take it easy. Okay.**

Commentary: The pastor is now understanding the emotional dynamics between Marshall and Lindsey. Marshall is evidencing grandiose entitlement and a lack of empathy for Lindsey. He is very angry at Lindsey for not "mirroring" him or giving him the adoration that he demands. These are essential elements of narcissism or what the Bible calls arrogant pride. Lindsey is a talented woman who apparently was taught in her family of origin that she was not of direct value but that if she could "marry a star" she would be validated or approved of at last. However, she seems sad, even depressed, and is probably turning her anger at Marshall inward upon herself. If she is experiencing vaginal pain on penile entrance as Marshall hinted, that may be an unconscious expression of her rage, a tightening of muscles and a blocking of vaginal lubrication. Both of these people are angry even though Marshall exhibits his by dominance and criticism and Lindsey attempts to hide hers even from herself though it shows physically and in her depression.

Pastor: Lindsey, I wonder how you feel when Marshall is so disappointed about sexual love with you. Will you tell me about that?

Lindsey: I guess so. I know he is right. A wife is supposed to want to make love with her husband, and I do! It's just that sometimes my body is dry . . . you know what I mean? And, it hurts when he enters me usually. I don't know what is wrong. My gynecologist says that everything is normal physically.

Pastor: I'm encouraged to learn that you are seeking help both with me and with your physician. With help I am confident that this is a solveable problem. If you are willing, please tell me something about how you feel when Marshall is disappointed about sexual love with you. Do you sometimes feel angry at him?

Lindsey: [glancing at Marshall, questioningly] Well, once in a while.

Pastor: Put some words to your anger.

Lindsey: Well, it's not that he does cruel things or is an alcoholic or anything like that. It's just that he doesn't understand . . . understand what it is like to be a woman.

Pastor: What specifically would you like Marshall to understand about being a woman?

Lindsey: We need—I need—closeness, closeness without sex: talking, sharing, Marshall being interested in me as a person and not just when he wants to have sex.

Pastor: How might Marshall show interest in you as a person?

Lindsey: Well, like I said, talking with me, asking me about my day, my problems, my feelings about things.

Marshall: I solve problems all day long. I'm president of my corporation. People come to me all day long and I've got to come up with answers. I'm not just interested in Lindsey for sex! I provide an income many times higher than most husbands. She doesn't have to work and she has everything she wants. That's "interest in her," wouldn't you think, Pastor? All I want is a little peace and quiet and some fun with my wife once in a while!

Commentary: The sexual problem for this couple is now fairly clear. They are both very angry and that inhibits their closeness. Lindsey is dependent on Marshall even though apart from him she is a competent, self-directing woman. At an inner level she probably is furious with him for blocking her career, for not esteeming her, and for blaming her for the problems in their marriage. Marshall is angry at Lindsey because he fears closeness and his anger helps him keep at an invulnerable and safe distance. As president he is invulnerable to his employees and deserves their loyalty. He believes he deserves Lindsey's loyalty. She exists to serve him. Since he has provided so well for her as an expression of his love for her, it seems to him to be outrageous that she is not a devoted (employee) wife. These two people will probably need long-term marriage counseling. They may do better in individual psychotherapy.

The problem near the surface here is sexual. The husband wants less conflict and more frequent intercourse. The wife experiences pain on penile entrance, vaginal dryness, and inhibited orgasm. However, the deeper root of these sexual problems involves severe relationship conflict because of the manner in which Marshall and Lindsey deal with anger. They will benefit much from learning new ways to be angry and new ways to be loving, powerful, and self-controlling (2 Tim. 1:7).

Other Relational Problems
Sometimes Expressed as Sexual Problems

A common marital problem involves the forty-five-year-old man who has been very achievement-oriented in his work. To reach his goals he neglected his family and arranged not to feel guilty about that by shutting down almost all his feelings. As a boy he was taught to "play through the pain." His father taught him to "be tough like me, not a crying wimp!" To gain his father's approval and a sense of manhood, he obeyed. Now forty years later he is in a midlife turning point because achievement is no longer fulfilling for him. Because he has largely shut down his feelings, his despair is hidden. He has no sexual interest in his wife. She feels unloved and depressed. At this point he may have an affair with a twenty-five-year-old as an escape from moving on to the next stage of his life: learning to feel and to make meaning based more upon relationships than upon achievement.

This couple may think that they have a sexual problem whereas they actually have a relationship problem of learning to share feelings and meanings. Both may need to study how Jesus was a person of many emotions. He wept, got angry, felt despair, was frightened, and became elated and excited. Part of Jesus' love was expressed through sharing his emotions. Also Jesus outgrew the achievement concept of masculinity. He achieved no social or business status, yet he found the ultimate meaning of life.

A different relationship problem that is evidenced sexually has to do with power or control. Which partner has the most power over the other? Randy had a very domineering mother and unconsciously is very determined never to be controlled by a woman. Sandra grew up with an alcoholic father and a dependent and stressed-out mother. Sandra took control of her parents' home to keep the peace and to try to keep Daddy from getting upset, drinking, and becoming drunk. Today she feels very anxious when she does not have everything proceeding in an orderly fashion. Randy is angry because he believes she is trying to dominate him.

These spouses do not trust each other's use of power. They compete for control. Randy may express the problem sexually by wanting intercourse when and where he wants it. Sandra may express control by refusing or by "having a headache" or by agreeing in a put down manner such as, "I'll be there in a few minutes as soon as I finish dusting the furniture." Their problem is not so much sexual as it is a failure to grasp the Christian concept of power as the energy for getting things done and the Christian warning that we are not to seek power over others (Mark 10:42–43).

Couples frequently complain that with the children, their jobs, and homemaking chores they are too busy and too tired for sexual love. They say they have no privacy for love making. He may be driven for professional achievement in order to prove his manhood. She may be a "people pleaser" who can say "No" to virtually no one because she believes that she must live up to the expectations of everyone. As a result, the only sex experiences may be late at night when the kids are asleep and they are very tired and hurried. They don't play or laugh or use incense or favorite music. They just have sex and go to sleep, and then not very often.

She may need to learn to say "No" as an expression of love for her husband, herself, and God. He may need to learn to accept himself as a man and then reduce his achievement drive. They may both be free to trade child care with other couples so that their kids are cared for on the weekend by others once a month. Then the two of them can be alone, rested, and ready to play and make love. Under these circumstances the two shall become one (Mark 10:8).

A common relationship problem expressed through sexual problems has to do with misreading each other's messages. She says, "I'm tired. I just need to relax tonight." He silently interprets this to mean: "She's down on me because I don't earn enough money so she could stop working. There's no point in my approaching her later for love making."

Or perhaps a couple misreads each other like this. He says, "How about my putting the kids to bed while you straighten up the house. Then we meet in bed for some lovin'?" She may silently think, "There he goes again, criticizing me for poor housework. I'm so tired of hearing that!" And, she says to him, "Knock it off, Jim!"

Many sexual problems are like an elevated temperature of a sick child. The high temperature is not the problem but an indication of a hidden infection. By asking spouses how they could get hurt or frustrated if they began to have lovely sexual passion, we may help them discover the hidden "infection." By asking people, "Emotionally speaking, what did you always want from your parents but had a hard time getting?" and then by asking, "How is your marital relationship parallel to that now?" we can help husbands and wives become aware of childhood messages that are currently hurting them. By asking spouses what they silently say in response to their partner's sex talk, we may help them become conscious of the ways some childhood experiences are inhibiting their God-given sexual joy in marriage.

Family-of-origin messages often interfere with married love when they are not replaced. Out of fear of rejection, spouses may set up defenses. These defenses will damage their sexual relationship. They may complain that their marriage is sexually "dead" when the actual problem is that they are still listening to some childhood messages about life such as: don't enjoy, don't be close, don't be sexy, don't be powerful, and don't feel. We can help couples "put away childish things" in order to speak, feel, and think like adults (1 Cor. 13:11).

References

Haskell Hirsch. 1988. *How to get the love you want.* New York: Henry Holt.

Aaron T. Beck. 1988. *Love is never enough.* Cambridge: Harper and Row.

7

Parents and Sexually Active Teens

Some of the most anguished moments pastors have occur when a teenager becomes sexually active and the parents or the teen seek help. If the teenager comes alone, not only are we anxious about the health, safety, and future of the teen, but we are also often torn over the dilemma of whether or not to tell the parents. If the parents seek counseling, they are usually quite distraught as they describe their suspicions or findings about their teen's sexual activity. We are "on the firing line" as we respond to these hurting people.

As we work together on pastoral counseling skills for effective help of such troubled families, we will suggest strategies for sex education, for working with the teen alone, and for working with the parents.

Sex Education in the Church

Our children need sex education at church! They are not receiving much help at school or at home. What they do learn is often from peers or from the exploitative messages of the media.

131

However, parents usually need help in being Christian sex educators; such sex education is needed by the time the child is two years old and annual parenting class can be very helpful. Church-related sex education must begin early in the child's life, at around ten years of age or just before puberty.

The most effective way to begin church-sponsored sex education with young children is to have special Bible study classes each year one evening a week for three or four weeks in hour and a half sessions. We do this class with fifth graders and their parents. We begin the study with a short welcome and general explanation that this special Bible study will focus on Christian understandings of our sexuality. Then the children go into an adjoining room for some activities. The other leader meets with the parents to explain the class structure and to deal with the parents' anxieties about the subject.

We then call the children back and begin by teaching, for about fifteen minutes, a biblically based view of one aspect of human sexuality. Then the group spreads out around the two rooms, sitting in family groups. In the family group the child can ask for clarification and the parents can talk much more openly about sexuality than they usually do at home. After about ten minutes we call the families back into the large group, answer questions, and then give a short talk on the next aspect of human sexuality. In an hour and a half, usually there is time for three leader talks and three family discussion sessions.

These sessions deal with God's creating us as sexual beings for love making in marriage. They deal with describing physical changes that occur at puberty and defining and repeatedly using words such as puberty, menstruation, testes, penis, vagina, and intercourse. The mystery of birth is described step by step from the perspective that in this event humans are sharing in the divine creativity of God. There are talks on sexual problems such as unwanted pregnancies, sexually transmitted diseases, and homosexuality. A presentation is also made concerning God's forgiveness of our sins, even sexual sins.

You may need emotional preparation in order to lead such sessions so that you will not be embarrassed and so that you will not talk down to the children. If you have difficulty with either of these usual emotional adjustments, it may be wise to scan your congregation for a school guidance counselor who could co-lead sessions with you. Your presence at the sessions adds much to the emphasis that God's Word guides us to beautiful and loving human sexual behavior.

These sessions are valuable. The children gain a Christian value-based view of God's design for human sexuality. They are much better prepared for the changes that will occur at puberty. And there is much more openness at home between parents and child for further processing of sex information.

We suggest strongly that you repeat the class for middle-school students and then again for high school students. Parents will not be involved in these classes, however. An entirely separate one-time meeting for parents before the classes for older students begin may help lower anxiety and provide parents an opportunity to suggest issues they wish to have discussed. We like the strategy of giving everyone a piece of paper and pencil and asking each person to write a question about sexuality he or she would like answered. Then we pass around a slit-topped box in which each person, parent and child, places the anonymous question. The questions may be answered at the next session or in the present session. The same question will, of course, be raised by a number of people and thus make the time required for answering them somewhat shorter.

Sex education is a continuous process because children grow and change and new children join the group. Repetition is also needed because the media message to "Do it, do it, do it!" never ceases.

For high school students you and the youth leader might watch for a movie that exploits sexual immorality and arrange to take teens to that movie. The group then returns to church afterward to analyze the subtle "brainwashing" techniques used both by the characters in the movie as they exploit each other and by the makers of the movie as they exploit the audience. In such training teens can learn to recognize false values and use Christian teachings to counteract them.

Middle school and high school teens taking part in a church youth program need some kind of repeated support for keeping sexual intercourse for marriage from this day forward. In an act of worship each teen might sign a pledge card and place it on an altar in a way that makes the dedication sacred. If a teen has already become sexually active, he or she can ask forgiveness from God in private or in a counseling session, and then use the phrase, "from this day forward." Because of the peer pressure and media pressure on teens today we believe that a ceremony of commitment is called for.

Our experience is that among church-going, baptized, Christian young people, about 50 percent are sexually active and regard sex before marriage as perfectly normal. They think three months is a long time to wait to have intercourse with a new date. Those who are still virgins in late high school begin to regard themselves as somehow sexually maladjusted. In this moral climate some teens claim that they do not feel guilty about their sexual activity and thus do not feel a need to be reassured that their sexual sins are forgivable. Others, however, are concerned with guilt and shame. They worry about the progression they see in themselves of having more and more sex partners. They feel shame about the tactics they have used to get sex from a reluctant partner. They feel chagrin when they break up and see the pain experienced by the person they have dropped. We must bring the gospel to all these young people both in terms of God's ideal about love, marriage, and sexuality, and God's readiness to forgive us and make us new creations with a new beginning (2 Cor. 5:17).

Pastoral leadership is essential in dealing with this issue. A pastor who is willing to listen to and learn from teens about their sexual values is by that action becoming qualified to speak to their needs. A pastor who is willing to invite the teens to reexamine their sexual ethics in light of their experience and their friends' experience will prepare the group for a dialogue about biblical insights and values about sexuality. When sharing scriptural insights, we should ask the teens to make practical applications rather than to preach informally to them about the text. We need to be patient with them when they disagree with us. We need not be embarrassed or corrective when they use sexually explicit language as they take part in group dialogue.

Jesus ministered in the marketplace and spoke with the people in their terms. Jesus asked questions, and he listened. His only stern lectures were addressed to the religious bigots of his day. He both ful-filled the law and held out forgiveness for violators. These qualities are essential in relating with teenagers about sexual matters. They need to hear from their pastors and their spiritual authorities, and they need to hear good news rather than embarrassed talk about inti-mate sexual matters. They will not be helped if we angrily denounce them or their sexual behavior. Surely love is the way of God.

Providing Accurate Information to Teens and Parents

Despite the so-called sexual openness our culture is now sup-posed to have, there is an enormous amount of inaccurate opin-ion current among both teens and their parents. Having sex edu-cation classes regularly at church and Christian sex education books in the church library can help. We have provided a list of such references at the end of this chapter. We will all be called upon again and again to help correct misinformation in our coun-seling sessions.

Pastors must be prepared to gently offer accurate information about AIDS and sexually transmitted diseases such as syphillus and gonorrhea. We need to be emotionally prepared to counter the erroneous beliefs of many teens such as that pregnancy cannot occur the first time a girl has intercourse or during her period.

We need to provide accurate psychological information as well. For example, there is a strong tendency for teens and adults to triv-ialize sexual intercourse the more partners he or she has had. Per-haps a fifteen-year-old believes she is deeply in love with the sev-enteen-year-old boy who is pressuring her. The decision to go ahead is a major turning point for her. After a few months they break up and she is devastated. Then she dates another boy and after a while they become sexually active. This decision is not as difficult for her to make. By the time she is a college sophomore she may have had seven or eight sexual partners, and going ahead with the next one is "no big deal."

Breaking up after being sexually active is much like divorce for married adults and teens have not lived long enough to be prepared for this level of grief. There is usually a long grieving process that may be self-medicated by a new sexual relationship. There is usually no family support for this grief as there may be in divorce because parents may not understand why the grief is so emotionally intense. Teens are simply too young to be "married and divorced"; they do not have the emotional experience necessary to cope with such losses without serious harm to themselves.

There are many nonloving uses of sexual intercourse at any age, but among teens this is especially prevalent. There is a strong tendency toward "power games." The boy may want a conquest either to boost his self-esteem or to brag about among his friends. The girl may want to hang onto the boy and give him sex in order to get what she really wants.

Being informed about sexual matters is thus a much broader topic than just dealing with God's direction for us and understanding anatomy.

Teens need help in learning about how to make Christian ethical decisions. Perhaps in your youth group there can be discussions about ethical principles many people use, such as hedonism, utilitarianism, the categorical imperative, and the biblical law of love. They might learn much from thinking through from each of these positions the decision to become sexually active. They need to learn to discern the ethical base being used by some media star, television commercial, or date. This decision will increase their power to resist making a poor moral choice.

Self-Esteem and Peer Pressure

A normal aspect of maturation is to move from seeking parental approval to seeking peer approval to eventually being mostly committed to self-approval as guided by God's Word. During the peer pressure period most of us make some hurtful decisions. Self-esteem is the basic essential for dealing wisely with peer pressure.

In a youth group program teens could be asked to focus on skills for building self-esteem. A warm-up exercise for the whole group could include asking what skills for self-esteem various people already know about and use. A question could then be asked about the logical fallacy of trying to build self-esteem on the approval of other people. Then the leader could explain that one way to build self-esteem is to enjoy and accept compliments given by others. One way to do this is to respond to a fine compliment by saying, "Thank you" and then saying silently, "That is true. I really *am* good at that!" The group could then break up into small groups to practice receiving and accepting compliments.

Back in the large group the leader could ask for some specifically Christian helps in self-esteem building. If members of the group do not think of these, the leader might list each of these methods: (1) We are valuable in God's sight because he gave us life, gifts, and calling to use those gifts in his service. (2) Jesus died for us because we are so valuable. (3) We are "God's kids"; we have been adopted into his family. God knows all about us and loves us and never gives up on us. (4) We can count our blessings and thank God for what is good in our lives and thus build positive attitudes and self-esteem. (5) We can take part in the church youth program and cultivate Christian love so that people build up one another instead of tear each other down as is usually done at school.

There are many other self-esteem building skills that you may want to suggest to teens. If they are to resist peer pressure and media brainwashing to become sexually active, they will need strong self-esteem.

If the church provides continuing sex education appropriate for both parents and youth and if the church helps families and youth build self-esteem, we may prevent some tragedies. People will have more spiritual resources for coping with the sex-related distress events that surely come to all of us.

A Pastoral Conversation

A fifteen-year-old girl approached the pastor just before the Sunday night youth group began.

Diana: Pastor, do you have a minute to answer a question? I'm kinda worried . . . about a friend of mine.

Pastor: Sure, Diana. What's the question?

Diana: Well, my friend, she is . . . sexually active, you know? And, she's afraid that . . . well . . . that she might have STD, you know?

Pastor: Yes. I can understand how your friend would be quite concerned.

Diana: Well, she wants to know whether or not if she sees her doctor and does have STD, will the doctor report on her to her parents?

Pastor's Silent Reflections: Oh, oh, this is no hallway theological question. What to do? Take her to my office for privacy? Assure her of confidentiality? Can I do that in this matter? Probably she is talking about herself, not a friend. First I need to build relationship here.

Pastor: Diana, that's a tough question because different doctors would handle it differently. How about coming down to my office for a few minutes to see what we can do?

Diana: Youth group supper is almost over and we start our meeting at 6:30. I could talk till then.

Pastor: Good. Let's go. [They go to the pastor's office and get seated.] I want to help, Diana. One possibility is that if I knew the girl's physician, I could call the doctor and ask what his or her policy is about confidentiality in such matters. Would that help?

Commentary: The pastor is moving strategically, dealing with one specific aspect of the overall problem. He is addressing Diana's felt need, how to get confidential medical care. By caring for Diana in terms of her need, the pastor is strengthening their relationship of trust and care. If he had focused on *his* need, to inform Diana's parents, he might have prompted her to break off this conversation.

Diana: Oh, yes! The doctor's name is Dr. Rankin.

Pastor: I've talked with her once or twice before. Suppose I call her tomorrow and get her answer about confidentiality? Can I then call you at home after school?

Diana: Yesss . . .

Pastor: But?

Diana: [smiles] Yes. Just please don't talk to my mother about this. She'd never understand.

Pastor's Silent Reflections: Since Diana readily knew the name of the physician, I am fairly confident that Diana is talking about herself. Diana has given me an opening to start work on the second issue, informing her parents, when she declared that her mother would never understand. I think I'll test the waters on that now.

Pastor: What would make it so difficult for her to understand in this matter?

Diana: Oh, you know. She just doesn't think teens are sexually active, doing it, much less know much about STD. I mean, we've been studying that stuff at school for years now.

Pastor: Suppose this person does have STD and the doctor can treat it. What then?

Commentary: The pastor asks a blurred question, not a sharp, invasive one. This makes it safer for Diana to answer because she can interpret the question any way she wants.

Diana: [long pause] Well . . . I'm not sure what you mean. [pause] My friend will surely hope she doesn't get STD again, if that's what you mean.

Pastor: Partly. And how will she feel about herself?

Diana: For getting STD? Well, she's sad and scared . . . and she feels all alone.

Pastor: I'd want to stand with you through all of this, Diana.

Commentary: The pastor does not directly expose Diana with this comment and yet does make it easier for Diana to open up about herself.

Diana: So, you figured out it's me? I . . . it's okay. Are you going to tell my mother?

Pastor: No. My concern is to stand by you and help. One way I could help is to meet here with you and your mother tomorrow after school and in that way perhaps you could both help each other. Will you do that?

Diana: I don't know. My mother will be so broken up. She'll be angry too . . . but here in your office she'll be on her good behavior. How did this ever happen to me!

Pastor: How about telling me about it?

Commentary: Diana opens the issue of how this could happen and the pastor follows her lead. Many of us who are patient in most counseling sessions tend to hurry in with our agenda when talking with sexually troubled teens.

Diana had dated Robert for about five months and was sexually active with him after a few weeks—her first experience. She had not yet told Robert that she may have STD. Diana felt some guilt for being sexually active but her primary concern now was STD. After a few more minutes they reaffirmed their plan to meet the next day and then stopped this session.

Commentary: The pastor is "tracking" Diana well in dealing first with the confidentiality issue both with the physician and with himself. Then he is dealing with getting the parents informed. He knows that soon Diana will be receiving medical treatment so that issue is covered. He did not get caught up in a sense of urgency that the parents be informed. There is time to talk and care and if Diana had wanted to meet with her pastor again privately, that would have been fine. The pastor also wants to help Diana avoid the consequences of sexual behavior. He does not preach at Diana nor does he push "his" issue as first concern. This is Christian compassion in practice.

The next day at 4:30 Mrs. Jackson and Diana arrived for the appointment. The pastor noted that Diana looked frightened and that Mrs. Jackson was embarrassed and puzzled. He guessed that Diana had not told her mother the reason for the session.

Pastor: Thank you both for meeting with me here today. I believe we can now talk openly and with love and solve the problem before us. Diana, are you ready to tell your mother the problem now?

Mrs. J.:   Oh! Are you pregnant? I thought something was going on between you and Robert! I told you . . .

Pastor's Silent Reflections: I need to empathize with her and protect Diana a bit too. Take it slowly.

Pastor: [interrupting] I can understand your apprehensions, Mrs. Jackson. It may not be as bad as you think [slowing his rate of speech as a way of helping Mrs. Jackson relax somewhat, the pastor then prepares the scene for Diana]. Let's just take it one step at a time and when you are ready we can hear what Diana wants to share.

Mrs. J.:   Let's hear it. I'm sorry. Honey, what's the trouble you are in?

Diana: Well . . . Robert and I have been . . . sexually active. But I'm not pregnant!

Mrs. J.: Not? That's a relief. [pause] Sexually active! I'm not surprised. That Robert has a lustful look in his eye. You're not the first he has taken to bed. [tears up] I just hate to see you hurt and ruining your life. What's going to happen to you?

Diana: Mother! I've not ruined my life and I'm not going to!

Pastor: [speaking slowly] Let's take one step at a time. You love and care about each other very much. You both have reasons to be scared and perplexed. I encourage you both now to draw upon your faith that God is with us here, now. By faith we can have the courage to solve problems and to learn from mistakes and build a better life as God leads us.

Commentary: The pastor does not divulge Diana's news, correctly discerning that this is for her to share when she is ready. Mrs. Jackson has not directly asked what the problem is, which indicates that emotionally she may not be ready to hear it. The pastor reminds them of a solid spiritual basis for hope and courage they both share. He is not hurrying them.

Pastor: Diana, I wonder if you are ready to tell your mother more about the problem now? Are you? If not, it's okay.

Diana: I'm ready. Mom . . . uhhh . . . I'm having symptoms. . . . I need to see Dr. Rankin. I think I've caught something . . . a sexually transmitted disease.

The pastor gives Diana a nonverbal affirmation for opening up, squeezing his two hands together, held up just a bit toward her.

Mrs. J.: Oh, that's *disgusting!* I never thought it would come to this: venereal disease! Well, why didn't you just tell me! We could already have you to the doctor.

Commentary: The pastor must make a judgment call here. The mother is critical as a way to deal with her own pain. If Diana needs some protection, the pastor would do well to speak up now. If Diana looks as if she can handle her mother, the pastor would do well to keep quiet and not "rescue" Diana.

Diana: Mother, I know you are disappointed in me. I am disappointed in myself. I didn't plan on telling the pastor about this. We just sort of met before youth meeting last night, and I gradually just opened up.

Mrs. J.:   We both know the first thing is to get you to the doctor. Then you'll have to tell Robert so he can get treated. I never want you to see him again, you understand?

Diana: Yes, Mother, I understand.

There was a bit more dialogue and both seemed ready to leave. The pastor gave some words of encouragement to both of them to love each other through this difficult time. Then he offered future help.

Pastor: Diana, if it is okay with you, I would like to meet with you here after school one day about two weeks from now, or sooner if you like. It might help if we talk about you and Robert and what you want to do in the future. Would you like to do that?

Diana: I think so. Maybe.

Pastor: I'd like to meet with you. Sometimes just being able to think out loud with your mother, perhaps with me, and maybe with your father, can kind of help foster sound thinking.

In a few moments the conversation ended. The pastor realized that there was much work to be done here. What is the involvement of the father? Is there an AIDS risk? Did Diana tell Robert or does she need some help with that? What does she plan to do about being sexually active? Can she become abstinent now? Would it be better to "face reality" and commit only to using a condom? The pastor had a time of prayer alone.

A Pastoral Youth Group Discussion

Perhaps you can identify with the pastor in this conversation. The youth fellowship met each Sunday night under the direction of church staff and volunteers. The pastor visited the group once each quarter to deal with issues that had been identified by the youth workers.

The pastor arrived early and greeted the youth. The president of the youth fellowship came up to talk more seriously.

Trish: We're all kinda sad and scared. Our friend at school, Carlotta, she's got HIV. She's a Christian and active in her church, but this happened, and we don't know what to think.

Pastor's Silent Reflections: This is more vital than the self-esteem work I had planned. According to Trish, this concerns the whole group. Go with the kids' felt need.

Pastor: What if we talk about this when the group convenes? Would that help?

Trish: [looking relieved] Yes!

A few minutes later the youth fellowship was convened. The pastor greeted them and chatted while they settled down a bit. He then began. "I am sad with you to learn that one of your friends at school has been diagnosed as having HIV, the virus that leads to AIDS. Perhaps there are questions you have and then maybe we could pray for her. So, what troubles you when you learn about this terrible struggle your friend Carlotta faces?

Charlotte: I just don't see how someone could be a Christian and be sexually active.

Pastor: [noting that several youth roll their eyes] Thank you for bringing that up. It is a difficult question. One way to begin thinking about it is to think how someone could be a drunk, a gossip, or a cheater in school, and still be a Christian.

Chris: Well, we all sin some of the time, I guess, so Christians sin, so Carlotta sinned I guess, but being a sinner doesn't mean you aren't a Christian—maybe just not a good Christian.

Pastor: Way to go, Chris! I agree with your statement that being a sinner doesn't mean you aren't a Christian. I believe I sin in everything I do every day.

Group: What????

Pastor: The word "sin" basically means to fall short of what God wants for us. I always fall short of God's standards. Perhaps you do also.

Mark: Well, then, if we're all sinful and if we are going to sin anyway, what's so bad about being sexually active?

Pastor: Good question. Since sex is great fun, how come God tells us not to do it outside of marriage?

Commentary: The pastor has been building relationship with the group up to this point by asking questions, by complimenting people who ask questions or give helpful answers. He is not lecturing, though that might be appropriate in another environment, or preaching, though that is appropriate in congregational worship. The kids are more relaxed and open now.

Mark: Well, you might get AIDS like Carlotta.

Chris: Or some other sexually transmitted disease.

Pastor: And . . . ?

Sherrill: A girl might get pregnant.

Pastor: Yes. There are many possible consequences when someone is sexually active outside of marriage. That's why God lovingly warns us not to do that. And there are other hurtful aspects to being sexually active before marriage. What happens to someone who has had eight to ten sex partners over a period of five to ten years?

Trish: Well, you could get a bad reputation.

Mark: Yeah, and you could get hung up with some bad characters.

Sherrill: I can't imagine having sex with ten people. [group laughs nervously] It makes me sick to think about it.

Pastor: Yes. Suppose a person who is a virgin is feeling pressured to be sexually active and that person agonizes over that decision for weeks. Then suppose he or she goes over the line and then later breaks up. There is a lot of emotional agony. Perhaps though, a month later that person starts dating another person. A few weeks later there is new pressure to be sexually active. Since this person is not a virgin any longer it is easier to say "Yes." After having had nine partners it may be no big deal to say "Yes" to the tenth. What do you think about that way of looking at things?

Sherrill: Makes sense.

Mark: I've got several friends at school who already have had—or so they claim [group laughs]—five or six partners. It seems like no big deal to them.

Pastor: And then there's the sadness and hurt of having an abortion. Have you had a friend share with you the heart-wrenching pain of having an unwanted pregnancy and knowing that marriage is out of the question and then starting to think and to pray about getting an abortion?

Charlotte: I couldn't do that. One of my friends has. She cried for days afterward.

Pastor:	That is very sad. [pause] Now, suppose you are being pressured to become sexually active with someone you really care for. How might you cope with that if you truly believed, as I do, that God's will for us is to save sexual love for marriage?
Trish:	You'd "Just say 'No.'"
Pastor:	Good for you, Trish. And what else?
Chris:	You could just say that you aren't ready for that yet.
Pastor:	Thank you, Chris. And how else could you remain true to your faith?
Sherrill:	You could pray about it and talk it over with a friend.
Charlotte:	But you could be very afraid you would be dropped. You know, all alone.
Pastor:	Yes, Charlotte. And how could you cope with that fear?
Charlotte:	I just tell myself there are other people to date and that I'm too young to get married now and I don't need to be with a guy who thinks that way about me. I mean, one guy, not here tonight, came on to me big time, but the more I listened to him, the more I realized he only had one thing on his mind. He didn't really want to be with me, he just wanted sex.
Pastor:	Great insight, Charlotte! Yeah. If someone is pushing you to have sex, ask yourself why this person wants sex with you. What is he trying to prove? What's she want that she's willing to use sex to get? Is he planning on bragging in the locker room? Is she trying to latch onto you completely? There are lots of motives for having sex besides making love. What are some other reasons why people pressure others to have sex?

Commentary: The pastor has helped many of these teens become more aware of motivations for sexual behavior. He ends his summary with a question, which is usually an effective strategy for encouraging listeners to think. The group could continue on in such a dialogue for forty-five minutes or so and then stop before it becomes too stressful.

We recommend that the pastor or other trained church leader engage in such sex-related group counseling work with senior highs on a regular basis. This will build rapport and help teens see the pastor as informed and approachable. They may then seek out private counseling with him or her. We cannot wait until the teen calls and makes a formal appointment for private counseling. That is too much to ask of most of them.

References

Terry Hershey. 1988. *Clear-headed choices in a sexually confused world.* Loveland, Colo.: Group Books.

Jay Kesler, ed. 1984. *Parents and teenagers.* Wheaton: Victor Books.

Josh McDowell. 1987. *How to help your child say no to sexual pressure.* Waco, Tex.: Word. (This is a book paralleling the video tape.)

Josh McDowell. 1987. *No! The positive answer.* Waco, Tex.: Word. (This is a video tape for youth.)

Josh McDowell and Dick Day. 1987. *How to help your child say no to sexual pressure.* Waco, Tex.: Word. (This is a video tape for parents.)

Male and female: Blessed by God. 1989. General Board of Discipleship, Division of Church School Publications, Nashville: Graded Press. (Curriculum for older teens.)

Our sexuality: God's good gift. 1989. General Board of Discipleship, Division of Church School Publications, Nashville: Graded Press. (Curriculum for younger teens.)

8

The Christian Ideal: Singles and Sexuality

In compassion for singles we may become so "understanding" of them in their struggle to date and to be sexually faithful that we tacitly give them "permission" to be sexually active with someone they are growing to love. We may also have a strong need not to be condemning. Part of our motivation for this "understanding" may be our need to be liked and approved. There are many motives that might prompt us to compromise our pastoral position and our own personal faith as well as to compromise our relationship to single persons. We think there is a better way.

We can uphold the biblical ideal without being self-righteous or judgmental toward sexually active singles. *The biblical ideal* for sexuality is that sexual intercourse takes place between two adults of the opposite sex who are faithfully married to each other and who both want to celebrate their love through touches, kisses, tender words, and love-play as they join in a "oneness" of mutually pleasurable sexual passion.

Yet *no one lives up to the biblical ideal!* All married people sometimes have sex to make up after a quarrel or to relieve biological

147

pressures or even as a bribe to get something else from a spouse. There is even marital rape in some relationships. All sexual activity in a Christian marriage is not biblical.

If then we are approached by a single person who is directly or indirectly asking how bad it is if he or she becomes sexually active, we can describe the ideal, admit that no one lives up to it, affirm that even inside Christian marriage there is sexual sin, and admit that outside marriage there is sexual love that somewhat approximates the ideal while still falling short of it. We can encourage the single adult to work to get as close to the biblical ideal as he or she can. Through patient dialogue in which we uphold the biblical ideal of sexuality and the forgiveness of God, we can minister to single adults as they confront their own emotional and sexual needs. We can identify with them in their deep emotional needs and their sexual frustrations. In our hearts we know that if we were single again we might not wait for marriage before having sex with a single person we love in a committed way!

The following three pastoral counseling conversations give examples of three different levels of need among sexually active singles. How might you have related to these three people?

Living Together Unmarried

A young woman approached her pastor late one afternoon and when they were comfortably seated in the pastor's office, she began.

Kate: I'm a Christian, have been since I was twelve years old. I'm twenty-three now. I've got a good job and my boy friend and I love each other a lot. He wants to get married, but I'm afraid or just sort of full of doubt. And well, I'm living in a way I said I never would.

Pastor: You two are living together but not married, is that what you are saying?

Kate: Yes. I'm not proud of myself and yet I love him and it would all be okay with me if we just went ahead and got married.

Pastor: Yet some fear holds you back?

Commentary: The pastor is listening patiently, asking questions without rushing in with any answers. This is the *Encounter* stage, and the pastor is building trust in the relationship.

Kate: Yes. I'm not sure what it is. I've never been married. He has. It was very painful for him—the divorce. I don't want that to happen to me. My parents never divorced, and yet I'm not sure they were ever really happy.

The pastor and Kate talked this way for another half-hour and then the pastor responded with a summary statement.

Pastor: Well, Kate, if I understand your dilemma, it is something like this. You feel regret about living with Doug and not being married to him. He is ready to get married, but you are not. You are held back by your awareness that a happy marriage is a very difficult goal to reach and you saw how little happiness your parents attained in their marriage. Is that about the way things look?

Kate: Yes! That's good. I mean that's clear, but it doesn't tell me what to do.

Pastor's Silent Reflections: I could meet my need to "play God" here. She's asking me to tell her what to do. I'm tempted. I'm glad it's no sin to be tempted. What can I do? I wonder if Doug would come in with her for a few sessions. She has said they are both serious readers; I could recommend Hendricks.

Pastor: Kate, I would like to make several very specific suggestions, if you want to consider them.

Kate: Oh, yes! Thank you.

Pastor: Well, my first suggestion is that you ask Doug if he would be willing to come in with you so that you could talk to each other about your decision with some help, perhaps from me.

Kate: He'd probably do that.

Pastor: My second suggestion is that you buy a copy or check out a copy from the church library of Harville Hendrick's book, *Getting the Love You Want.* It is a wonderful book designed to help couples uncover hidden agendas in their relationship so they can consciously make choices about how they will care for each other. There are sixteen exercises at the end that you could do together after you read the book.

Kate: That sounds interesting. I'll write down the name so I don't forget. You say the book is in the church library?

Pastor: Yes. One other suggestion is that you make an appointment with me now for you and Doug to come by one day next week to build relationship and to discuss the basic idea of the book. Then when you finish the book and the exercises, if you still have troubled doubts, we three could meet again two or three more times.

Kate: Yes. We'll do that. Let's make an appointment now and then I'll go down to the church library.

Commentary: This is a sound example of bibliotherapy. The pastor has read a book that speaks to the needs of this couple. He determines that they are readers and likely to read the book if he suggests it. He plans for follow-up with them after they have read the book. The pastor was not judgmental about Kate and Doug living together outside of marriage nor did he implicitly or explicitly tell her "not to worry about that little problem." He has held up the biblical ideal and has helped prepare them to consider moving much closer to that ideal.

Not Making the Same Mistake Again

Esther had now been divorced about a year and had started dating. She had served on several church committees and had also turned to the pastor while going through the anguish of her divorce and recovery. Her ex-husband was highly narcissistic. He was handsome, glib, and an effective salesman. Yet he had no sensitive ability to tune in to the inner being of anyone except himself. He had gotten into several affairs during their marriage and finally left Esther to marry one of his girl friends.

Esther asked for an appointment because she had met a man she was strongly attracted to and with whom she was seriously considering becoming sexually active.

Esther: I'm glad you could spend time counseling with me. You helped me so much last year going through the divorce. I never, never want to hurt like that again!

Pastor: I believe you have grown a lot and have become a much wiser woman because you went through that suffering. What seems to be your concern now?

Esther: Well, I mentioned to you on the phone that I've met a guy, Randy. He's handsome, successful, been single about three years now, and we're seeing a lot of each other. We haven't gone to bed yet, but my heart pounds when he touches me. He's not pushing me, but he really wants to make love with me. He's a Christian, and he thinks sex is okay if the two people are committed to each other. But he's willing to wait. I still kinda think it's not okay until you are engaged with a wedding date set, you know?

Pastor: I know you have thought long and hard about the biblical ideal of sexuality. I am confident that you want to be true to your faith.

Esther: Yes. [pause] Well, that's about it.

Pastor's Silent Reflections: What's happening? She was animated; now she's shut down somewhat. Did I say something that's troubling her? I think so but I haven't the foggiest notion what. Ask her gently!

Pastor: Esther, I've a hunch that something I've said is disappointing to you. If that is so, will you please tell me what?

Esther: Well, it's just that . . . Well, I know you are against premarital sex and I hear you telling me that's what I'd better believe also. I guess I do believe it but I don't think I can live by that ideal.

Pastor: Oh, now I think I understand. When I said, "I am confident that you want to be true to your faith," that put pressure on you to live up to that ideal. Is that it?

Esther: [shy smile] Well, yes! I mean, I don't expect you to tell me to go to bed with Randy or that it's okay. Still, I need your support for whatever I do.

Pastor: Esther, I believe you are a fine Christian woman. You are one of God's people and if you do go to bed with Randy or someone else, you will still be one of God's people and I will still admire you as a fine Christian.

Esther: Well, thank you. I'll try not to go to bed with Randy no matter how much my heart pounds when I'm with him. How I'm going to control myself, I don't exactly know.

Pastor: What strategies have you thought of so far?

Commentary: The pastor's encouragement for Esther to think specifically about methods for reaching the goal actually helps her be more alert and effective in managing her emotions. Abstractions such as "I will do better" are only a small step forward. Descriptive specifics help much more.

Esther: Well, I'm praying about it. I'm talking with you. I'm talking with Randy, too, and praying with him about it.

Pastor: Good for you. What control do you use about where you and he kiss and hug?

Esther: Huh? We kiss and all but we don't touch each other too closely.

Pastor: I'm sorry, Esther. I didn't word my question very well. I'm wanting to suggest that another way to exercise control over passion is to avoid kissing with a bed very nearby.

Esther: Oh! [laughing] Now I understand. That was funny. Well, we kiss in my living room and in the car and at the front door. He's never been in my bedroom and I wouldn't go into his. With my feelings so strong that would be basically a decision to have intercourse with him.

Pastor: I agree. Put two fine people in a tempting situation long enough and any of us are very likely to go over the edge. I encourage you to continue to pray and talk and to avoid intimate locations for passionate kissing and holding. [pause] Esther, I'd like to get back to another aspect of this issue that you mentioned at first today.

Commentary: **The pastor is using fine listening skills, recalling the broad agenda here, not just the last topic mentioned.**

Esther: Sure, what is it?

Pastor: You mentioned that you were really afraid of ever being hurt again like you were with Robert [first husband]. So when you take a close look at this handsome, successful, and talkative man, in what ways does he resemble Robert?

Esther: Oh [looks down] I hadn't thought about that. And yet that really is what is on my heart. They are a lot alike: handsome, talkative, good "sellers," both Christians.

Pastor: And what was the big thing that was missing with Robert that caused you both such agony?

Esther: Well, Robert, he was . . . is . . . so lacking in care for anybody but himself. He was really gallant or thoughtful toward me when we were dating but a few months after we were married, he just went on to other concerns. Or at least that's the way I felt. It's as if he wasn't able to understand why being faithful to me was so important to me.

Pastor: So he could size people up, say what they wanted to hear, but mostly just to get what he wanted from them, whether it was a sale or marriage?

Esther: Sure! That summarizes him very well.

Pastor: So do you know Randy deeply enough to size him up in that regard?

Esther: He seems attentive. So did Robert. I don't know.

Pastor: Are there any clues for you in knowing what went wrong in his first marriage?

Esther: He's told me a little about that. It was very rough for him. She got depressed, began to drink a lot. I don't think there was another man.

Pastor: What's your hunch about why she drank so much if she was married to such a handsome, successful husband?

Esther: I don't know.

Pastor: That is something you would do well to check out with Randy. Also, how does he treat you in little ways when he is not "on stage"? Does he seem to believe that he is supposed to choose which restaurant you go to or does he order his favorite for you? Or does he get irritated when you don't agree with him?

Esther: Now I'm more worried. In a way I don't know the answers to your questions, but I believe I need to focus on those issues for the next few dates. Robert did all those things early on and I didn't see what that meant. I actually don't think Randy is as self-centered as Robert, but I need to see more, hear more.

Pastor: Good for you. Keep your eyes open. And, conversely, let him know your "dark side." We don't have to be cynical to be shrewd.

After a few more minutes Esther and the pastor ended this conversation. Esther was much more equipped to relate to Randy now. First, she felt affirmed that it was too soon to get sexually involved with him. Second, she was more aware of the biblical ideal for sexuality. Third, she was much more alert to the possibility that her heartfelt arousal around Randy could be a danger sign. Perhaps Randy was a lot like Robert. If so, she could not make a fine marriage with him unless they did a lot of psychotherapy together first. She was now committed to avoiding intercourse with Randy and to observing him and asking him questions to uncover the degree of his self-centeredness. She was also prepared to reveal to Randy more of what about her contributed to the break-up of her marriage to Robert. Perhaps in several months Esther and Randy will know each other much more at a heart-to-heart level and will then be able to decide whether or not to continue their relationship and perhaps to consider marriage.

I'm Just Not Ready to Be Committed to Marriage

Sometimes we stray far from God's ideal and at other times we get only into some shades of gray. In pastoring people in difficulty, one consideration is to assess how far from God's ideal the individual is. Another consideration is to assess the readiness of the person to grow from confrontation. Narcissistic people, those who suffer from what the Bible calls "arrogant pride," will very often just break relationship with anyone who confronts them. We can still help them by giving encouragement when we can and by asking questions that may help them confront themselves. The following, all too typical, pastoral counseling relationship illustrates this difficult work.

Carl attended worship regularly and served on church projects at times. He was a talkative and outgoing person liked by everyone. He went through a very painful divorce and during his grief had some counseling sessions with his pastor. His ex-wife, he stated, was very inhibited, bossy, and critical, just like his mother. He became depressed; she got on his nerves. After twelve years of marriage he had an affair that lasted six or seven months. He broke it off without his wife finding out. A year later he had another affair, and when his wife learned of this, she divorced him.

As the pastor and Carl met one evening before a church committee meeting, the pastor asked, "Hey, Carl, how're you doing?"

Carl: I'm doing okay. Got a little something I'd like to talk over with you sometime. Maybe I could see you in your office like I did last year?

Pastor: Sure. You want me to call you at work tomorrow and set up a time?

Two days later they met. Carl seemed relaxed and happy. He was self-confident again.

Carl: I sure feel a lot better now that I'm not married to Clara. I know divorce is wrong and all, but I was really miserable with her. And yet I just thought that was what a man was supposed to put up with.

Pastor: You missed out on a lot of joy, I believe.

Commentary: The pastor is in the *Encounter* stage, even though they did some counseling work a year before. He does not agree that Clara was a bad wife because Carl would interpret that to mean that the marital problems were all her fault. The pastor does affirm that Carl missed out on a lot of joy.

Carl: Yeah. She was never satisfied. I couldn't please her. Well, I've met someone I like a lot. We've been dating a couple of months and she's getting serious. Every time she mentions marriage, I panic a bit.

Pastor: You were hurt so badly before that just talking about marriage makes you uneasy, is that it?

Carl: Yeah! I mean, don't you think I ought to take my time and not get married until I feel ready?

Pastor's Silent Reflections: What is going on here? He's met someone, that sounds okay. She is getting serious. He's scared. That doesn't quite warrant getting back into counseling. He doesn't sound as if he's grieving over Clara. He seems open with me, that's good. Theoretically he wants support from me to stay away from marriage until he feels ready. There is something else. I imagine he is sexually active with this woman, maybe that's it. He's not bringing that out though. Fears my confronting him?

Pastor: I agree that you do well to avoid getting into an agreement to marry when you are just not ready for marriage yet. How come the woman is pushing you to get married?

Commentary: The pastor asks an indirect question that still invites Carl to open up the issue if he is ready. This is less confrontational than a direct question: "Are you having sex with her?"

Carl: Well, she says she likes me a lot and she knows I like her. I guess we do love each other, some. And, well . . . she's very sexy.

Pastor: So, if you are having sex together, that may explain part of her desire to get married.

Commentary: The pastor does not accuse Carl of being sexual with the woman. He uses the word "if" and then invites more sharing on a very important issue: understanding the woman he's dating.

Carl: Yeah, I think so. I've been with three or four women now since the divorce, single women, you know, and as soon as sex starts they start talking marriage.

Pastor's Silent Reflections: Carl is still very self-centered and shallow. He doesn't experience women as whole persons, and yet he is so attractive that they are drawn to him anyway. If I confront him about his shallowness or his having sex with three or four women over the past eighteen months, he'll get huffy and leave. The best I can do is to affirm him and then invite him to grow.

> **Pastor:** So as you become more and more understanding of the women you meet, what is your understanding now of how come they start talking marriage as soon as they become sexual with you?
>
> **Carl:** [grinning] Well, they sort of think of sex and love and marriage going together, I guess. That's Christian, I know. And they don't want to get VD or have their reputation ruined.
>
> **Pastor:** I agree with you. What is it like for this woman you are seeing now, to be so intimate in sexual intercourse with you even though you don't have the intimacy of marriage to support your relationship?

Commentary: The pastor did not pick up on Carl's reference to his behavior as less than Christian. There was an opening and yet perhaps the pastor knew that going into that now would only lead to an argumentative dialogue.

> **Carl:** Oh, I don't know. I don't see what you mean.
>
> **Pastor:** I did ask a long question there, sorry. [smiling] What I'm wondering is, how might this woman hurt when she opens herself so fully to you and you won't commit to her?

Commentary: The pastor handles his error graciously; he models for Carl that being in error is a mistake and yet not necessarily something shame-ridden.

> **Carl:** Well, I guess she feels like I don't value her . . . but I do! She's really nice looking, intelligent. We have great fun together.
>
> **Pastor:** So she knows she is intelligent and attractive and fun to be with and then she gives you sex and you don't want to think about marriage with her. What does that mean to her inwardly?
>
> **Carl:** [frowning] That I don't like her . . . but I do!

Pastor's Silent Reflections: He is little able to tune in to her. He hasn't even used her name yet. Perhaps I need to refer him for long-term psychotherapy. He certainly looks very narcissistic to me.

Pastor: Well, I'm willing to guess what she might be feeling, but I don't know her. Do you want to hear my guess? Well, she knows she's attractive and intelligent and sexy and yet you don't want to talk about marriage. She may begin to feel that you just want to be with her, play with her, use her for your happiness, and then drop her when you are through. Could she possibly feel that way?

Carl: Well, yes. Kitty—that's the girl I was with a few months ago—accused me of feeling that way. Made me mad.

Pastor: Thank you for sharing that with me. I can understand better now and perhaps encourage you more as you figure things out.

Commentary: The pastor is deliberately not confronting Carl but is encouraging him to grow in empathy or understanding compassion for the women in his life. Such growth might lead to more moral and more loving behavior.

Carl: [frowning] So you think I've got a lot of growing to do before I can marry anybody!

Pastor: Well, yes. When you become more compassionate toward women, they will trust you more and then, I believe, you will meet someone you will want to marry.

Carl: No sex before marriage, huh!

Pastor: Well, that is part of God's ideal for us. And yet another part is that we have compassion for one another, really understand what makes one another tick. That is a vital part of love and marriage.

Carl: Thank you, pastor. I've got to go now. [grinning] I'll let you know when I meet someone I want to marry.

Pastor: I'm happy we could talk man to man like this. Keep on growing and come by to share like this anytime.

Commentary: The pastor puts a positive interpretation on Carl's walking out when the talk was more than he was willing to face. This may help Carl return for more work when he is ready.

Pastor's Silent Reflections: Well, I probably didn't serve you well in this one, Lord. Carl didn't grow much in that conversation. I feel like I've lost a battle if not a war. I thought my confrontation there at the end was very gentle but it was more than Carl could handle.

I guess I did help Carl stay in touch with the Christian ideal about sex even though he didn't like it. Dear Jesus, how would you have handled this talk with Carl?

Conclusion

Our ministry to singles regarding sex may involve affirming some for living out the value of no sexual intercourse outside of shared, committed love in marriage. At other times we may work with singles seeking forgiveness for sexual mistakes and grief they are experiencing. On other occasions we may be in the difficult role of listening to someone describe sexual behavior that we believe is unfaithful, damaging to those involved, and will lead to even more suffering. We cannot change anyone except ourselves; all we can do is patiently love and listen and gently interpret. We can affirm God's ideal for sexuality without condemning anyone. We are not spiritually qualified to "throw stones." Perhaps in that graceful environment God's love and the person's distress will lead to motivation and power for the person to change and grow.

Reference

Harville Hendrix. 1988. *Getting the love you want.* New York: Henry Holt.

9

Strategic Pastoral Counseling with Survivors of Sexual Abuse

There are many different forms of sexual abuse that are likely to come to your attention over the years of your pastoral career. Think back over the people you have known and cared for who have been raped or who as adults have reported to you that they were sexually abused as children. Or perhaps you recall some distraught person telling you of the present ongoing sexual abuse of a child. The gospel has much power for healing such people when we are prepared to become involved in that process through sharing the pain of the survivors and even of the perpetrators.

In this chapter we will describe the most typical needs of people in this form of distress and then outline what you and others can do to help bring God's love to them.

Survivors of Incest and Other Childhood Sexual Abuse

Current sociological data suggest that about 20 percent of all girls and 5 percent of all boys are sexually molested or abused at

159

least once. One recent study conducted among 643 members of the Christian Reformed Church found that 13 percent of this sample had experienced sexual abuse.

There are degrees of such trauma ranging from teasing sexual "humor" about the child's body, sensuous caressing, fondling, oral sex, intercourse, offering the child to others for intercourse, and satanic ritual abuse of the child by members of a cult. These tragic crimes are committed by Christian, middle-class, educated people! Those who have perpetrated these crimes or who have been victims and survivors of these crimes are very likely to be people in your congregation next Sunday.

The effect of these crimes upon the survivors is influenced by many variables. The severity of the sexual contact is one. Whether it occurred repeatedly is another. Whether the perpetrator was a parent or a family friend, a member of the extended family, or a stranger strongly influences the degree of betrayal the survivor will likely feel. The age of first occurrence is also a major factor. The availability of other adults who heard the child's complaint and took appropriate action influences the degree of long-term harm. Many of those with whom we have worked report that a parent, teacher, or pastor did not believe what the child reported and that that betrayal made the trauma much worse. Several survivors even reported that they were sexually abused by their pastors after they reported they were being abused at home.

When the world turns out to be such a terribly unsafe place in which there is little or no protection, the child feels much like a combat soldier. Some of the symptoms of adults who have survived sexual abuse in their home exhibit many of the symptoms of post-traumatic stress disorder (PTSD). These signs include intrusive "flash-back" memories, recurrent nightmares of the events, a sudden emotional surge as if the event were occurring in the present, a hyperalertness for danger, intense reflexive responses to appropriate but unexpected touch, sleep problems, chronic guilt, and high anxiety whenever the individual is in an environment like the one in which the crimes took place.

The horror of repeated sexual abuse is so great that many children repress all memories of these events. Years later, often when their own children are in danger from the same perpetrator such as their grandfather, mothers begin to have flashbacks revealing the crimes committed against them. At first, they may believe that they are becoming mentally ill since these unbelievable pictures are coming into the mind unwanted. Gradually they accept the reality of the crimes committed against them.

Another pattern seems to be that after these women have reared their children and have reached middle age they can be poised and powerful enough to face their tragedy. They are no longer new brides and they no longer have small children. They have proven their adult capabilities by making a home and helping their children have a good start in life. They have given their children what they, themselves, so longed to receive. Now they are empowered to care for themselves. In this new safety, their unconscious mind may begin to bring these childhood horrors to consciousness.

Another pattern in this problem is that many women survivors of childhood sexual abuse become promiscuous as teenagers or young adults. It is as if they believe they have no value except as sex objects. They are also usually acting out their hatred for men in this behavior. When they marry, they often unconsciously choose husbands who will sexually abuse them in marriage and thus repeat the childhood trauma. Then they further blame themselves for what has happened to them.

Other women become very sexually circumspect, even prudish, as adult women. They may have much difficulty being sexually responsive in marriage even though they want to be with their husbands. Some women unconsciously become obese as a result of two factors. First, they may use food as a form of love: "I am hungry for love so I will eat food." The more emotionally distraught they are, the more they eat as an addictive act or a form of self-medication. A second factor is that being obese is a hoped for protection against having men come on to them sexually. The fat is a kind of body-armor.

The Law and Abused Children

If you are dealing with a minor who is reporting sexual abuse, you are likely to be required by the laws of your state to report the abuse immediately to the state authorities responsible for children.

You will probably be able to do this anonymously if you wish. Our suggestion is that you make contact with an attorney and ask to have state law explained to you in the light of confidentiality commitments you want to make to people.

If you report the abuse, a parental offender will likely be taken from the home, perhaps put in jail, and the children will be exposed to more pain as social workers come into the home and ask questions to determine whether or not in fact sexual abuse did occur. If you do not report the offense, you may be breaking the law and the child may feel deeply betrayed and unprotected. More abuse may follow.

Sometimes there are alternatives, though they are very difficult in terms of the Christian ethic. You may want to consider talking privately with the perpetrator, and if he or she confesses and commits to not being abusive again and enters professional counseling immediately, you may commit yourself to not reporting the abuse for now while maintaining close contact with the person's therapist. You can make it clear that any hint of further abuse means that you will most certainly file a report.

It is vital that a condition of your holding back on reporting is that the perpetrator enter into psychotherapy immediately and that you be in telephone contact with the therapist to determine whether or not the perpetrator is continuing in therapy. Perpetrators are likely to lie about and repeat their crimes and also to lie about their therapy.

The professional you involve may feel compelled to report and your efforts to keep the matter private will be ended. Perhaps the professional will also agree to withhold reporting to see what can be done. Be aware that these decisions to not report are probably against the law in your state and such a decision can be validly made only on the basis that: (1) we have reliable bases to believe the abuse has stopped; (2) the perpetrator is alarmed and will not act again; (3) the other parent is fully aware of what has happened; (4) the child is protected both by receiving counseling and by being reassured that if anything abusive happens again, he or she is perfectly free to report it; and (5) reporting would lead to destruction of home and marriage because of imprisonment and scandal. One way to check all this out is to call the anonymous hotline in your state for child abuse situations and discuss these options.

There will probably be no legal issues involved in your arranging for counseling for the child and the nonabusive parent. In terms of human love and well-being, that help is the first priority.

Rape Survivors

There are some similarities between the long-term emotional damage done to rape victims and to child sex abuse survivors. Rape survivors will also likely exhibit the symptoms of PTSD. They will probably be reluctant to prosecute because that means answering very intimate questions and reliving the event many times during the trial. Rape victims are also quite likely to be blamed for "getting themselves raped."

You may be called to visit a rape survivor in a hospital emergency room. The rape crisis counselor affiliated with the police department may call you to become involved if the woman tells her that you are her pastor and are a strong source of support. You may be in counseling with a woman working on low self-esteem or generalized sexual inhibition in marriage, when suddenly she wonders out loud if any of this could be caused by something that happened years ago that she has kept secret. She may then describe date rape in college or high school. She may tell about being raped by her husband's best friend. She may hesitantly suggest that her husband has raped her. She will have opened up a terrible wound and a heartfelt opportunity for a deep level of spiritual healing.

There are many forms of spouse abuse and yet all such acts have a similar tragic outcome: they seriously damage joy in the relationship for both the perpetrator and the survivor. There may be physical abuse that involves hitting, choking, pushing, and destruction of favorite things belonging to the other person. There may be sexual abuse such as mate rape. Some spouses force the partner to take part in sexual acts that the partner does not want or enjoy such as mate swapping, anal intercourse, or bondage activities. There may be emotional abuse like yelling, cursing, calling the partner ugly and demeaning names, engaging in a continuous critical harangue, and belittling the partner in front of extended family or children.

When one or both partners engage in this level of relationship-destroying behavior, professional counseling help is urgently needed. Most large cities have shelter homes for spouses and children when someone in the home is being abusive. You as a pastor can help survivors of such abuse find shelter services and make contact with an appropriate counselor for help. It is vital that we convey hope to abuse survivors because many of them have been "brainwashed" so that they now believe there is no hope that they can resist or get out of an abusive relationship.

Individuals abuse others in the home for many reasons. The most common aspect of the pattern of abuse is that usually abusers were themselves abused as children and watched one of their parents abuse the other parent. Abusers often have extreme power or control needs and are driven to dominate their partners. Most abusers have unconsciously transferred rage at a parent onto their spouse. Virtually all abusers and survivors have an intense fear of closeness, and the abuse creates emotional distance such that neither individual must face his or her own inner dark side in confession and repentance.

One couple approached their pastor for counseling. He knew them well. He had performed their marriage ceremony four years previously. They both regularly attend worship services. Both are professionally employed and are the parents of a two-year-old girl who is in the church preschool program.

Pastor: Come in. Have a seat. I am glad you have decided to come in to share something of what you are facing. Will you each begin perhaps by giving me a brief sketch of what prompted you to come in?

Brenda: Well . . . uhhh . . . I insisted that we make an appointment. Something's got to change. I know I am going to change myself and I hope Clark can handle my becoming the kind of woman I intend to be. Pastor, I have come to see over the last year or so that I have been a dependent sort of woman at home. I first got my eyes opened when I worked for a man who was critical and demeaning toward me every time he opened his mouth. I put up with it at first, telling myself he was the boss and could get away with behaving like that. Then I got so tense I decided that I would get a different job even if it meant less pay. Actually I ended up in a better job. That accomplishment stirred me up so that I began to look at the same pattern in our marriage. Clark, you are a good man in many ways and I want our marriage to work but I am no longer willing to put up with continuous crap from you. Pastor, he controls both our paychecks. He has been making me ask him for spending money. I am opening a separate checking account in my own name today where I will deposit my paycheck. And, Pastor, there are other problems. He seems to crave any sexual act that I tell him I do not like. It is as if he enjoys forcing that on me. And, well, what actually drove me to call you yesterday was that three nights ago he—well, he raped me! [begins to weep] He wanted *sex*. He didn't want *me*. I told him "No" and he kept on coming at me. He choked me, threw me on the bed, made me have sex with him. That's rape, and it is never going to happen to me again!

Pastor's Silent Reflections: Good for you! When I first went into the ministry women wouldn't have felt free to do anything to help themselves in these "family matters." This *jerk* calls himself a Christian and treats his wife like this! Wait a minute. Take it easy. Where's the intensity of my anger coming from? Clark is one of God's people and I am as big a sinner as he is. Be gentle. Build relationship. Clark is not going to get help if you shame him.

Pastor: Clark, I imagine this is very painful for you also. Will you tell me how this looks from your point of view?

Clark: Sure. She's exaggerating, that's all. Sure I got irritated with her for giving me a hard time but I didn't choke her. I mean, I just held her by the neck as I pulled her down on the bed so we could get on with it. We've always been a little rough like that. I thought she liked it. She had never said anything about it before. Heck, if she wants me to take it easy with her from now on, that's okay with me.

Brenda: I don't believe you! I can't trust you. Tell the pastor the truth!

Clark: I am, woman! Shut up! You and those stupid women libbers! Why can't you just be good wives instead of making all this trouble?

Pastor: Please, let me interrupt for just a moment. I'm wanting to understand each of you as best I can. If you will each just let me ask a few questions that will help me understand more deeply the painful trouble you both are having. Now, Clark, if it is okay with you, would you please tell me about your home as a boy?

Clark: Sure. What do you want to know?

Pastor: Thank you for being willing to be open with me. So, please just tell me about things like what happened when you were a boy and your parents were having a disagreement.

Clark: Oh, well, not too much. They got mad like everybody else. Dad would yell at Mother and us kids, when we were out of line. He never beat her but of course he pushed her some, to get her moving, and she cried a lot and that used to drive him up the wall. They got a divorce when I was about ten or eleven. I never saw much of him after that.

Pastor: So, what part of your father's style of relating to your mother do you want to copy or keep in your relationship with your wife, Brenda?

Clark: Well, he worked hard, he drove a semi-trailer all around the state, delivering stuff, you know? He went to church with her every Sunday.

Pastor: I can see that you would want to follow his example in those ways. What about his style with your mother do you intend not to follow with Brenda?

Clark: Well, I don't want our marriage to end up in divorce.

Pastor: Is there anything else about your father's behavior that you do not want to copy?

Clark: Well, I don't really want to yell at Brenda. I know I get out of line a bit with her at times. I do it in spite of myself, you know what I mean?

Pastor: Sure. I have my own problems keeping my promises to myself to improve my relationship with my wife.

Clark: Well . . . uhh . . . do you have any suggestions about how I could work on some of this stuff?

Pastor: Yes, I can suggest some methods you might want to use to change yourself. Is that what you want to think about now?

Clark: Yeah. Sure. [relaxing, speaking more softly and slowly; rapport is now fairly good]

Pastor: Well, suppose you wanted to go one week without getting angry at Brenda. There are two strategies you might want to use to reach that goal. The first would be to set up some kind of a reminder of your goal such as all the time you are at home, wear a rubber band on your wrist. Every time you see it you can then remind yourself that you have decided to go one week without "snapping at" or getting angry at Brenda. The second suggestion that I would make is that you use the concept, "Thinking causes feelings." If Brenda buys a $75 dress without checking with you first, you could think to yourself, "What? She spent $75 on a lousy dress! Why if she keeps that up we will be bankrupt before we know it!" If you thought like that you might well feel anger. If instead you thought to yourself, "She needs to look sharp in her work. I like the way she looks. She must have thought about it and have decided we could afford it," you might feel enjoyment of her attractiveness. Does that make sense, "thinking causes feelings"?

Clark and the pastor continue in dialogue about these two behavior modification skills and Clark seems willing to learn and change. The pastor realizes that he needs to stop the session in a few more minutes so he turns to Brenda.

Pastor: Brenda, how do you feel, hearing Clark work to learn and grow this way?

Brenda: I feel a lot better than when we came in. I have some hope. Clark, I will do what I can to help, but I see this is your work and I do hope you use the skills the pastor has taught you.

Pastor: And, Brenda, what are you willing to change about yourself to make your marriage happier?

Brenda: I'm going to become a more independent and powerful woman. I am going to protect my boundaries. Clark is going to have to adjust to that.

Pastor: I understand. In God's design, Christian marriage is made up of two whole people who freely choose to enter into a marriage oneness. The woman is not inferior to the man nor is he to her. I encourage you to keep on developing your authentic power, not power over other people but power for being the best you can be in God's service. What are you willing to change about yourself this week that would probably bring more delight into Clark's life?

Brenda: Well, right now I'm still somewhat angry at him so I am not willing to do much. I will tell you one thing I will do, provided he makes the change he said he would here today. He really likes turkey and dressing and pecan pie. Clark I'll make a fancy meal like that for Saturday night if you would enjoy that.

There is more dialogue about the meal and the reality that each of these people is willing to change and grow not only to save their marriage but to become more fully the people God created them to be. The pastor then asks them if a closing prayer would be helpful. They both say that will be very helpful. He asks them how they would like to pray. Brenda says she will pray and commit herself to being cooperative with Clark. Clark says he would rather pray at home. The pastor then says he will close the prayer after Brenda prays. They then close the session this way and schedule an appointment for the following week.

Commentary: The pastor helped these two troubled people ventilate their anger without letting them escalate to the level of rage. He monitored his own hostile reaction to Clark and kept that from intruding on his counseling relationship. By the middle of the session he did not feel hostile toward Clark. Surprisingly, Clark readily agreed to make some changes. The pastor wisely then invited Brenda to consider making some changes. She needs to make changes for her own well-being and by both of them agreeing to make changes, Clark has not become the "identified patient" or the one to be blamed. At the beginning of this session there was considerable evidence that these two people would require referral to a marriage counselor and that there might be little hope they could remain married even after that work. By the end of the session there was evidence that Clark was willing to change and Brenda was willing to work with him. These two people will still need a great deal of assistance from the pastor over the months ahead and yet with five or six sessions now and then a monthly meeting for a year or so may well be able to build a new life within a Christian marriage.

Specific Strategies for Helping Sex Abuse Survivors

During the *Encounter* period of the first and second sessions you will do well to be gentle, soft-spoken, and affirming of the person for sharing with you and with God this horrible experience. It will likely be appropriate not to ask about other sexual trauma until the person has much of the story out in the open.

During the *Engagement* period of the second through fourth sessions you may want to outline specific steps the individual may choose in order to further the healing process. These steps may include memory healing, "doing the thing you fear," forgiving the perpetrator, "forgiving" God for not protecting the survivor from the attacks, and taking charge of her own body again.

In memory healing we may want to point out to the individual how Jesus helped Peter heal the memories of his denial that he ever knew Jesus (Luke 22:54–62; John 21:15–17). Jesus helped Peter relive that awful experience and to do so in the presence of Jesus' love. In similar fashion we can ask people to pray that Jesus' presence will be especially felt now. As the person relaxes and trusts more, the person can relive the experience. She or he may need to relive the experience several times in the presence of Jesus before the pain is reduced to levels that he or she can manage. Often, we need to face such horrors from our past in order to be free to live life abundantly in the present.

The counselee may need to learn some deep spiritual strategy for becoming profoundly relaxed such as centering prayer. He or she can then go back to the places where the abuse occurred. He or she may need to take a trusted Christian friend. Driving to the old neighborhood, parking in front of the house where it happened, and then being deeply spiritually centered, helps the individual grow in a sense of power. No longer a victim but a survivor, she or he is a person who has faced the tragedy and is now in charge of the memories instead of being haunted by them.

There is much forgiveness work to be done by most survivors. A girl may need to forgive her mother for not discerning what her father was doing and for not protecting her from him. If her father was the perpetrator, she may be unable to pray to God the Father and may need to pray to Jesus or to the Lord. She may need to "forgive" God, not in the sense that God sinned against her but that she cried out to God over and over to "make him stop it" and God never did. She may need to forgive herself for not finding a way to make the perpetrator stop even though that is an unfair guilt burden for her to impose on herself. We as pastors may be reluctant to encourage this aspect of forgiveness for fear the survivor is taking responsibility for the perpetrator's act. We can question the person's motives until they are clear to both of us, and then we must follow the lead of the individual.

The last and most difficult person to forgive is the perpetrator. Sometimes asking God to forgive the perpetrator is a first step of this stage. The survivor must understand that forgiveness does not mean to explain away; rather Christian forgiveness involves a cross. We experience the pain of the crime committed against us and then we forgive. One strategy is to write a letter to the perpetrator outlining the crimes committed and then stating that forgiveness is hereby given. Even if the perpetrator is dead or unknown, writing a letter helps make the act of forgiveness concrete.

If the perpetrator is alive there can be great healing power for the survivor in writing a letter asking for a joint meeting in the presence of a counselor for the purposes of declaring what happened and for reconciliation. The survivor must be prepared to feel powerful and healed even if the perpetrator denies everything and thus blocks reconciliation.

Once a person has relived the crimes committed, forgiven the persons involved, and has begun to have an attitude of, "Thank God, I survived!" she or he may be ready to "take control" of her or his own body again.

Perhaps she was a child when the crimes were committed; now she is a powerful adult. Perhaps she was not able to stop the crimes until she left home as a young adult because she was so under the "spell" or deep control of the perpetrator; now she is a powerful adult. As a powerful adult, no one can touch her or use her body in any way she does not choose. God has given this body to her, not to her perpetrator! In the privacy of her own home she may need to touch her body in sensuous ways and affirm during that touch that "This is my breast (abdomen, pubis, thigh) and I enjoy touch that I choose." More and more she will become poised and assured that she is a survivor, not a victim, and that this is her body, not something her perpetrator can ever possess!

Survivors of childhood sexual and physical abuse as well as rape usually need two to four years of psychotherapy to attain healing. Not only will they need such time to work through the PTSD problems, but they are likely to also suffer from multiple personality disorder. These kinds of deep needs call for the assistance of a professionally trained person who can give such lengthy care. During such long-term therapy, you as pastor can help by occasional phone calls, notes, and face-to-face talks. Your task in such contacts is to give support, being clear that taking such a long time to heal is a measure not of the counselee's failure, but of the enormously outrageous crimes committed against her. Her persistence over such a long time in therapy is evidence of her courage to face her pain.

Examples of Effective Pastoral Counseling with Survivors

A married couple came to their pastor's office by appointment and declared with some tension, fear, and anger that sexual abuse had occurred.

Ruth: My daughter came to me Sunday afternoon and told me that . . . this is even hard for me to say. Jim had caressed her sexually the day before as they swam in our pool.

Pastor: I'm saddened with you all. Jim, would you be willing to tell me what happened?

Jim It's true. [weeping, hunched over, looking at the floor] I didn't mean to do anything hurtful and I didn't put my hand inside her, or even inside her bathing suit. This is terrible!

Pastor's Silent Reflections: His body language seems to indicate anguish, guilt, sorrow; that is a sign of hope. He mentioned putting his hand inside her and that probably indicates he was tempted to do that or else he would not be denying it now. Let's see, their daughter Mary is eleven, and if so she may be able to recover from this horror—*if* this is a first time—which I doubt!

Pastor: Yes, Jim. This is terrible, painful. I can imagine something of your pain as well as Mary's and Ruth's.

Jim: I don't know how bad off Mary is. Ruth will probably never be able to forgive me. It's not that we have a bad sexual relationship in our marriage. I don't know what made me do it.

Pastor's Silent Reflections: He is presenting this as if it only happened once. I am skeptical. What personality traits made him vulnerable to doing this? This is going too fast. I need to slow down the work.

Pastor: Jim [in a slow, deliberate voice], how about telling me a little more about your marriage and how you and Ruth usually deal with things?

Jim: Well, we've been married thirteen years. Mary is eleven and Jimmy is nine. We both grew up in the church. Ruth is a great wife; she is always there to do what I need from her. [Jim goes on for several minutes. He is more relaxed to be talking about more pleasant aspects of his life. He is growing more hopeful as he talks.]

Pastor's Silent Reflections: Jim appreciates Ruth for what she does for him. He may not see her as a person in her own right. She seems to have been content to be his aide and to put down her own needs. There may not be much of "two people making a oneness" here.

Pastor: Thank you, Jim. I can see that you and Ruth have much to be thankful for. Ruth, what might you add to what Jim has shared with me thus far?

Ruth repeated some of what Jim said, and felt more "into" and not left out of the dialogue now. The pastor spoke in a similar tone, volume, and rate of speech as Ruth and this helped rapport. All three were now sitting in a more relaxed manner.

Pastor's Silent Reflections: There is at least one more thing I need to know. Is this a one-time event? They seem to be more trusting now. I think I can safely ask.

Pastor: Jim, if you are ready, please describe to me other sexual contacts you have had with Mary.

Commentary: This is a leading question worded in such a way as to assume that there have been other contacts. Such wording usually makes it easier for a person to tell more of the truth if he or she has done so previously. The wording implies that the questioner already knows the truth.

Jim: [glancing quickly at Ruth, an indication that what he is about to say will disturb her even more] Well, there hasn't been much else except, well, we sometimes wrestle. I've rubbed her bottom and she giggles. Well, actually probably two other times I have caressed her the way I did in the pool. [glances at Ruth again]

Pastor's Silent Reflections: There may yet be more of these events. I need a private session with Jim so he will be more able to open up. Ruth looks even more distraught now.

Pastor: Ruth, this must be very difficult for you. What might you need from Jim or from me just now?

Ruth: Just pray for us. I don't see how I can ever trust him again. I don't think we can ever get over this.

During the next two sessions the pastor heard both people. In a private session, Jim seemed very congruent in stating that he had had no other sexual contacts with Mary or any other child. The pastor decided not to report him on the basis that the contacts had been rather mild; Ruth and Mary had a clear understanding that Mary must tell her mother if anything else happened; Jim seemed contrite; and Mary might feel to blame if the marriage came to an end because of police or human services investigations. Toward the halfway point of the fourth session the pastor started working to make a referral.

Pastor: You have unburdened yourselves here and seem to feel a ray of hope through confession and asking God's forgiveness. I believe, Ruth, that you are not far from being ready to forgive Jim. Jim, I believe you when you declare that you will never touch a child sexually again and that you will call me if you find yourself even tempted to do so. I believe that you would do well to have some Christian marriage counseling over the months ahead and that Mary would benefit from talking with a Christian woman counselor about reaching puberty, sexuality, growing up, and what has been done to her in this matter. Without mentioning your names, I have talked over your situation with Dr. Rebekah Ashley, a Christian friend to whom I have referred other people who have benefited from her help. She is willing to work with Mary and you. How does it sound to you both to see her for a while?

Jim: Oh? Well, I guess so. I just thought that you could help us.

Pastor: I am committed to helping the three of you. Referral means calling in additional help, not my dropping you from my care or my prayers. What I am suggesting is that you see Dr. Ashley and then have a fifth session with me. You may recall that I mentioned that five sessions was all I was prepared to do with you at this time. In that fifth session we could evaluate how your session with Dr. Ashley went, pray together, and set up a means for being in contact in the months ahead. Now, how does that sound?

Jim: Well, I guess so. Isn't that usually very expensive?

Ruth: [interrupting] It's what we need to do!

Pastor's Silent Reflections: Good for you, Ruth. Mary is a bit safer now if you are going to be assertive. Why is Jim so reluctant?

Jim: Okay, okay. I'll go . . .

Pastor: Jim, let your "inner child" speak up and tell me what is the most frightening aspect of your seeing Dr. Ashley?

Jim: Oh, I don't know. [pause] It's just that I'll have to go through it all again and it's so embarrassing.

Pastor's Silent Reflections: He's embarrassed at what he has done, at getting caught; he's not showing much empathy for the damage he has done to Mary and Ruth. I need to alert Dr. Ashley to possible serious character defects.

Pastor: Embarrassing?

Jim: Yeah. I did something bad. I know it. Now I'll have to tell it to some stranger who probably won't give a hang for me.

Commentary: This man feels like a "bad *boy*" and he seems to fear that this woman, Dr. Ashley, won't love him like a *mother*. This suggests that he may have a longstanding wound in relation to his mother. This is "transference." That may underlie his sexual abuse of his daughter. For Jim to become quite reliable in no longer being a danger to his daughter, he will need to work through whatever his hidden childhood issue is.

Pastor: That will be hard. No doubt about it. I'm believing that you have the guts to face up to it and take action.

Commentary: The pastor is not falling for a possible trap by defending Dr. Ashley, the "mother figure." He is not criticizing or threatening Jim for his reluctance to enter psychotherapy. He is appealing to a strength in Jim's self-image, that he is a man and can take action. This is very effective encouragement for Jim to now do his best.

Jim: Yeah. I Will! I'll see this Dr. Ashley.

Pastor: Good for you! I'll look forward to getting your impressions of her
            after you have seen her a few times. Now, we have a plan. You will
            see Dr. Ashley. I will contact her with the information you have given
            me. After you have seen her two times, how about giving me a call
            so we can set up a follow-up visit here? Now, I'd like to offer up a
            prayer for you. Would that be okay?

            Dear Heavenly Father, we thank you for your love and hope and for-
            giveness so freely given to us when we sin again and again and again.
            Please help Jim to face like a man what he has done and to learn and
            grow into an even finer person. Please help Ruth search her heart for
            readiness to forgive Jim, for wisdom to help in the healing of Mary,
            and for power to assert herself truly in life. And, Lord, we pray now
            for Mary. Please help her to be healed and then prepared for her ado-
            lescence and womanhood. Please help me to love Jim and Ruth and
            Mary in warmth and understanding in these months ahead. In Jesus'
            name we pray, amen.

The pastor may be consulted by individuals already in psychotherapy, who want encouragement and answers to their spiritual questions about their experience. These people want us to listen and care and not to rush in with answers. They will want us to
know something of the stages through which they are moving from
sexual abuse toward healing. They will be reassured to learn that
we have some training for working with them on these issues.

They will want us to affirm that they were not responsible for
the crimes committed against them. They will need assurance that
they are still valuable persons to God, much wanted as a part of
the church fellowship, and not dirty or defective. They may want
to know why God let the perpetrator continue such awful behavior. They may want to ask if they must forgive the perpetrator and
how they can possibly generate the will to forgive.

Survivors will likely become quite depressed as they face the horrors they experienced. They may become suicidal. They need someone to turn to for a "life link" or for protection from their own
despairing feelings and their fear of committing suicide. While the
therapist carries much of this responsibility, as pastor, you can be
a vital source of God's hope so that the individual can remain in therapy and work toward healing. You may have a healed survivor in
your church who would also be available to give assurance and

hope. Survivors need to hear again and again that remaining alive and gaining healing is important to God and to the individuals giving reassurance. They need to hear that we are confident that they and God have the power to endure the pain until healing is accomplished. The pain of facing these horrors of childhood is enormous and requires many months of work. Over this period of time survivors need repeated assurance. The need may stir up feelings of impatience and despair in us, and this is our problem to deal with in consultation with a friend or in prayer. The victim-becoming-a-survivor needs us to give in warmth and conviction repeated assurance of God's love and hope.

References

Dan B. Allender. 1990. *The wounded heart, hope for victims of childhood sexual abuse.* Colorado Springs, Colo.: Navpress.

Peter Nicolai et al. 1991. *Report of Synodical Committee on physical, emotional, and sexual abuse (SCONAB) in the Reformed Church.*

Basil Pennington. 1982. *Centering Prayer.* Image Books.

David A. Seamons. 1985. *Healing of Memories.* Victor Books.

S. and S. Simon. 1990. *Forgiveness, how to make peace with your past and get on with your life.* New York: Warner.

10

Strategic Pastoral Counseling with Homosexuals and Their Families

W ith much hesitancy someone may have confessed to you, "Pastor, I'm a homosexual. I hope you won't tell me I am going to hell." With similar pain and shame you may have had a father and mother pour out to you in anguish, "Our son has just announced that he is homosexual! Pastor, where did we go wrong?" Since research studies generally indicate that about 2 percent of Americans are homosexual, there are people in your congregation who may soon tell you that this is a problem for them or someone in their family.

We invite you now to consider research findings about the nature of homosexuality, biblical teachings about this behavior, and then pastoral counseling responses you may want to make.

Causes of Homosexuality

There is a growing interest in medical research to determine whether there are genetic causes of homosexuality. Recent autopsies of homosexual men and heterosexual men have uncovered several differences. One finding was that a lobe of the brain was smaller in one group than the other. Another finding was that an endocrine gland in one group was larger than in the other. Both these differences make the homosexual's brain structure somewhat more like that of women than that of men. Perhaps more differences will be found in the future.

Despite these findings, there is no conclusive evidence at this time that homosexuality is biologically *caused.* The differences found already may indicate a biological *influence.* We do well to make a clear distinction between cause and influence. A man with high testosterone levels will be hormonally influenced to be more aggressive. He still has choices as to how he expresses this biological reality. He may become violently aggressive or he may achieve much by working more assertively in his profession.

Another way of seeing the difference between biological cause and biological influence is cited in the research findings that if one identical twin is homosexual, the odds are 52 percent that the other will be homosexual. Among fraternal twins the rate drops to 22 percent. Some 11 percent of genetically unrelated (adopted) brothers will become homosexual if the brother is homosexual (Associated Press, December 1991 Archives of General Psychiatry). If homosexuality was *caused* by genetic factors the rate for identical twins would be 100 percent, not 52 percent.

All questions on this issue are certainly not answered at this time. However, the findings at present seem to suggest that homosexual identity is learned just as heterosexual identity is learned. No one is born homosexual though some are born with biological influences that will make it easier for them to choose homosexuality. No one is born heterosexual though most are born with biological influences that make it easier for them to choose heterosexuality. Future research findings may confirm this position or require revision.

There are also psychological influences on all of us in our choice of sexual orientation. Male homosexuals usually grow up in a home in which the mother is overly invested emotionally in the son and the father is in some way distant. The father may be angry, critical, and domineering. The father may be living in another city and is seldom seen. The father may be present but severely noninteractive with the son. Effeminate characteristics in fathers have not been shown to influence their sons to become homosexual.

Once a boy recognizes that he is a male who will become a man, he usually finds models of masculinity in his father and in other men such as a teacher, pastor, uncle, or coach. Having many models helps him compensate for whatever deficiencies he perceives in his father. However, if the boy does not bond with his father or a father substitute, he may not bond with other father figures either. Then he may be more likely later to develop homosexual behavior. Unconsciously, he seeks a deep caring from a male or father substitute. If the search for male bonding becomes eroticized, such as by receiving warm, male, acceptance from an older homosexual, he may begin to develop a homosexual orientation.

Female homosexuals usually grow up in very difficult relationships with their mothers. Again, however, the father is distant and unhelpful. It is as if two-year-old girls decide that they do not want to be like their mothers and yet they long deeply for heartfelt nurturance and acceptance from their mothers. Later, after puberty, as they experiment with lesbian behavior, they are actually seeking feminine bonding they never had with their mother. It is as if by having sexual passion with another woman with much touching, they are at last being "nursed," caressed, and desired by "mother."

Homosexuality usually takes on the characteristics of addiction. Over time, sex usually becomes the center of the homosexual's life just as alcohol or cocaine may become in another person's life. A strong tendency is established to use sex as a kind of self-medication. Whenever the homosexual person is emotionally distressed by such experiences as work disappointment, fear of illness, or rejection by a friend, he or she may seek sexual experience in order to obtain a chemical high to mask the emotional distress. Such experiences actually release in the brain a chemical much like morphine, called "endorphin," which does create an emotional high. Gradually, having a normal homosexual experience is not enough, and so there is a tendency to "increase the dose" first by more frequent sex and then by increasingly dangerous sex. After a few years, the homosexual may be having many anonymous sexual contacts where the danger is high and thus more endorphins are released.

Research has also uncovered indicators as to which individuals are more likely to be able to change their sexual orientation with professional psychotherapy. A highly motivated person in his or her early twenties is more likely to be able to change than an older person. Success is also more likely if the person has had fewer homosexual experiences. People over thirty-five who have had extensive sexual contact are much less likely to be able to change orientation though they may be able to attain celibacy. The more traditional values they have, the more likely it is that homosexuals can change orientation. Furthermore, they will likely do better working with a therapist of the same sex; this is especially true of male homosexuals.

Often the individual who seeks help is in his or her mid-twenties and can no longer tell people that his or her friend is just a roommate. Parents are urging marriage. Developmentally, the individual is longing for much more heart-to-heart intimacy with another adult. The choice of sexual orientation must now be made. Often at this stage the individual makes some attempt in seeking counseling help.

Biblical Teachings about Homosexuality

First, God loves homosexuals as well as heterosexuals. We are all saved by grace, not by works or moral merit. Homosexuals can be Christian just as can arrogant pastors or gossipy lay leaders or alcoholics or those who snarl at their spouses rather than "speak the truth in love."

Second, we need to be careful that we do not condemn in others what we are refusing to face in ourselves. All of us have had and may still have some hurtful sexual problems. Homosexuals provide heterosexuals with scapegoats (Lev. 16) onto which they can project their own dark side. However, when we are judgmental toward others we bring God's judgment upon ourselves (Matt. 7:1). So as a spiritual discipline we need to be alert any time we are harsh or punitive toward some sinfulness in others. We need to ask ourselves, "How am I guilty of or tempted to do what I condemn in others?"

Third, the Bible clearly teaches that homosexuality is sinful. Leviticus 18:22 and 20:13 declare that it is an abomination to God for a man to be sexual with another man as with a woman. In the New Testament Romans 1:24–27 clearly describes homosexual behavior and declares it sinful. First Corinthians 6:9–11 declares homosexual behavior to be sinful. (See also 1 Timothy 1:8–11 and Jude 7 for further statements on the issue.)

To help us maintain perspective, let us remember that the Scriptures also declare that gossiping is sinful, and we are all guilty of that. Adultery is sinful, and surely all teens and adults are guilty of that (Matt. 5:27–28). Homosexuals are sinful. Heterosexuals are sinful. "All have sinned and fall short of the glory of God" (Rom. 3:23). We are all saved by grace through faith not of ourselves lest we should boast (Eph. 2:9). So, we Christians live in joy because of God's gracious love and hope for us.

When we err, we become more aware of that and then learn more about the way of God. When we confess our faults to God and share our struggles with other Christians, we are empowered anew by God to make both heartfelt character change and outward behavior change. God stands ready to forgive us, love us, and help us learn and grow.

We believe it is important that the pastoral counselor identify with his or her homosexual counselees, recognizing that we are all sinners seeking God's way. We will not be able to minister to homosexuals if we distance ourselves from them such as by silently exclaiming, "Well, at least I've never done that!"

In the practice of Christian psychotherapy we have seen homosexuals who have changed their sexual behavior and identity. Some of these people were male and some female. We have also known that many consider attempting the change and then decide not to do so. I (Harold) have an ex-client who sends me a Christmas card each year with a news note about she and her husband. She usually sends a photograph of her two children. When I met her she was struggling to go on living because her homosexual lover of four years had rejected her. She decided to change her sexual orientation and did so after much courageous effort on her part and some pastoral counseling work on my part. The book by Nicolosi cited at the end of this chapter provides more scientific data that homosexuals may change orientation if they strongly desire to do so.

With Parents of a Homosexual

Father: Pastor, we are devastated by some terrible news. I can hardly bear to tell you what has happened. Our son tells us he is coming out of the closet, or whatever they call it. That he is *gay.* We are just destroyed by all this. He says he doesn't want or need counseling and that we must just accept him as he is.

Pastor's Silent Reflections: Think! I didn't count on this to come up with these people today. What do I need to get clear in this *Encounter* stage? How much time do I have now to care for these people? I've got to be at the hospital in two hours so I can do forty-five minutes now and then schedule more time tomorrow. Do I need to alert my secretary to stop all calls? Yes. What has been my relationship with Jim [the father] prior to this? Jim has been a somewhat angry and critical lay leader; he's usually pretty sure he is right on things. He doesn't let anyone get close. He must be hurting something awful to share this with me. I need to go very slowly and build relationship with him. One slip and he may angrily dismiss me. I'll think about the son later. Jim is my concern now. I hardly know Mary. She seems downcast, ready to follow Jim's lead.

Pastor: Jim, I hurt for you! This has got to be a terrible blow.

Jim: Yes! What did I do to deserve this? I've done everything I know to do to set a Christian example for Harry and now this. [tears up]

Pastor's Silent Reflections: Jim needs to cry but probably fears he will feel humiliated to let me see his weakness. I need to affirm his manhood.

Pastor: Your tears express your love for Harry; please let them flow. I'm encouraged that you can share feelings with me man to man.

Jim: It's rough. I can't sleep. There's just got to be something I can do about this.

Pastor: You love Harry with all your heart.

Jim: Yes, I do. I don't know how I can go on loving him while he lives with that disgusting faggot!

Pastor's Silent Reflections: Jim may want to blame Harry's lover in order to avoid blaming himself. We are too soon into this to ask him to face that now.

Pastor: Loving someone often means heartbreak too.

Jim: It sure does. Pastor, what are we going to do?

Pastor's Silent Reflections: **He's more relaxed now, more open. Mary hasn't said anything, so perhaps now I can approach her.**

Pastor: I don't know, Jim. I do believe God will help you grow in hope. Right now I need to understand more of what is happening. Mary, how are you dealing with all this?

Mary: I'm very sad. He'll get AIDS and die! He'll never have children. It's like everything is coming to an end.

Pastor's Silent Reflections: **She sounds depressed, talking about everything coming to an end. Is she suicidal? She's probably grieving both over the news and over the loss of a dream of being a grandmother.**

Pastor: What kind of feelings are you having about just giving up, quitting?

Mary: Well, I'm mostly still kind of numb, in shock. I thought my kids were grown and didn't need me anymore and now Harry has this terrible problem. I don't know if I can stand it. I just wish I could escape.

Pastor's Silent Reflections: **Mary has not been much involved in women's activities here. I hardly know her. Jim is so dominant. She may have missed out on a lot of love and joy. She has put up with a lot, I suspect. She and Jim may have more severe marital problems now because they are both so distressed and neither has much comfort to give the other. This may be a turning point where she gets some help for herself. Still, I need to check out the suicide potential a bit more.**

Pastor: When you want to escape, how do you cope with thoughts about suicide? [pastor notes that Jim looks at her with alarm and even a touch of anger]

Mary: I just push that out of my mind.

Pastor: If you were going to end your life, how might you do it?

Mary: Oh, I don't know. I haven't thought about that. I don't want to do it. I don't want to go to hell.

Pastor's Silent Reflections: **I'll not tamper now with her belief that she will go to hell if she commits suicide. She doesn't have a** method chosen so I think the suicide risk is low enough for now but I will need to watch that.

Pastor: Mary, will you commit yourself to call me and talk, anytime day or night, if you start thinking very seriously about ending your life?

Mary: Well, I'm not going to do it.

Pastor: I understand, yet if you will I want you to make the commitment to talk with me if ever you feel yourself getting close to that, will you?

Mary: Yes.

Pastor's Silent Reflections: She still hasn't made a clear commitment.

Pastor: Will you tell me your commitment?

Mary: If ever I get close to doing myself harm, I will talk with you first.

Pastor: Thank you, Mary! I am encouraged by your commitment. Now I will need to stop in a few minutes and so I would like to make some suggestions. Will you both set a time to meet with me tomorrow or the next day and talk more? Are you willing to do that?

Jim: We could come by after work, say around 4 tomorrow?

Pastor: [checking his calendar] That is okay with me. Is that okay with you, Mary?

Mary: Yes.

Pastor: Good. Now, I have this booklet that deals with sexual problems from a Christian perspective. It has one chapter on homosexuality in it, only about eight pages long. Would you take this and read that section before tomorrow afternoon?

Mary: Yes. I'm glad you have something like that for us.

Pastor: All of us from time to time get very badly hurt and need to turn to God for hope and courage. I have certainly prayed in anguish in my own life quite a number of times. I wonder now if we might need to have a time of prayer together about all this?

Jim: Yes! Let's pray for Harry to come to his senses!

Mary: I'd like that. We all need God's help.

Pastor: How might we pray together now that would be most helpful to you both? Holding hands, kneeling, standing? Would you like to pray aloud and then I'd close, or some other way?

Jim: Well I'll pray and then you could pray . . . and Mary could pray if she wants to. I guess we could hold hands, if you want to.

Pastor's Silent Reflections: Well, he almost left Mary out but at least he didn't speak for her. It's going to be tough for him to open up enough to let God help him, I'm afraid. I'll look at Mary to invite her to speak for herself.

Mary: I'll pray for Harry also.

Pastor's Silent Reflections: They might focus only on Harry's needs and not on their own.

Pastor: Suppose each of you pray for Harry and for yourselves to have patience and courage and hope and then I'll pray with you both. [reaching out to join hands in a circle]

Jim: Dear God, please help Harry come to his senses. He's a good boy. He doesn't deserve all that's going to happen to him. It's that disgusting creep that's done this! Help us to lead Harry to change and get out of this mess. Amen.

Pastor's Silent Reflections: Yes, it's okay for me to intuit issues in other people's prayers! I'm not criticizing. I'm listening lovingly. Jim seems to feel anger, disgust, and tenderness. I'll include that in my prayer.

Mary: Dear Jesus, Harry is a good boy. We love him so much. Please help him to get the professional help he needs and please help us to have the strength to carry on.

Pastor's Silent Reflections: Mary prayed to carry on, to resist suicide, and she affirmed her love for Harry. She prays to Jesus, Jim to God.

Pastor: Dear Lord Jesus, we open our hearts to you in prayer knowing that you love us and understand us and have hope for us even when we are discouraged ourselves. I pray for Jim and Mary now that they will feel, O God, your loving power filling their hearts so that they can cope with what lies ahead. And we three gather in your name to pray for Harry that he will believe in his heart that you love him and will help him become a finer and finer Christian and that he can change his sexual orientation. In Jesus' name we pray, amen.

I'm grateful that we have had time together. I'll need to stop now, though. Are we all set for 4 P.M. tomorrow?

Jim: Sure. We need your help to find a way to help Harry.

Mary: Yes. Thank you. We appreciate your help for us very much.

Pastor: Thank you. I'll look forward to meeting you here at 4 P.M. tomorrow and I'll continue in prayer with you all through this time. Goodbye for now.

Mary and Jim leave and the pastor sits down at his desk to make some notes.

10/12/94 Jim and Mary Smith came by unexpectedly, report that their 19 year old son, Harry, has announced he is a homosexual. Jim is angry, disgusted, and sad. Mary is also very sad, somewhat suicidal, no method chosen. Gave them sex prob bklt. Jim has attempted to control everything and this is beyond his control, tough for him. Mary seems passive, depressed, probably punishing herself for failing somehow. Next: 4pm 10/13.

Commentary: The pastor has now established a trusting, working relationship with these two hurting people. His focus has been on them and their needs at this time. In the next several sessions the pastor will need to hear Jim and Mary, pray with them, answer their questions, and recommend to them several Christian psychotherapists who can work with Harry if he wants help now or in the future about his sexuality.

As we resume this case summary Harry refused to see the pastor or be referred for psychotherapy, and the pastor was meeting with Jim and Mary for the fourth time.

Pastor: You both seem to be adjusting to your distress about Harry and that is in itself an act of faith. You both are "taking up the cross daily" and that is one way to love Harry between now and the time when he wants help.

Jim: Do you think he will ever want help?

Pastor: I believe so. Homosexual relationships are notoriously short-lived and when Al breaks off with Harry, your son may hurt so much that he will say to himself, "No more," and want help. I encourage you to wait in love until Harry "comes to himself" much like the prodigal son. If you hassle him about therapy he may develop even more resistance. In the meantime let us all be in prayer for Harry even as we also pray for you two. So suppose we have an understanding that we won't schedule any more appointments for now, but that if there is some change we will get together again. Is that okay?

Jim: Yes, Pastor. Thank you for your help. When we came in here we almost thought it was all over. We both feel better now.

Pastor's Silent Reflections: Jim still speaks for Mary. I need to check her out and ask her to reaffirm the no suicide commitment. I hate to bring that up, but it's necessary.

Pastor: Good for you both! Mary, how do you feel about not scheduling any more times together for now?

Mary: You have really helped us. Thank you.

Pastor: I'm glad I could help. Mary, one more question. Are you still committed to calling me if you get so discouraged that you start to think seriously about taking your life?

Mary: Oh, I haven't felt like that now for a week or two.

Pastor: I'm encouraged to hear that. Will you remake the commitment?

Mary: [smiling] Sure. I will call you if I start to think seriously about killing myself.

Pastor: Thank you. Perhaps now would be a good time to have prayer together. How would you like to pray this time?

Again, after Jim and Mary leave, the pastor made some process notes. It might be six months or more before he hears from them again and he will need his notes to help himself tune in to these two good Christian people in need.

Being with a Troubled Homosexual

A year later the phone rang and Harry introduced himself.

Harry: My parents tell me that you were a great help to them last year. I need some help. I've not been to church much the last four or five years, and I really don't need to be preached at or anything for who I am. Do you have anything that might help me?

Pastor's Silent Reflections: I don't know what has happened here. Harry may be asking for a counseling appointment or a referral. *Relationship* is the first thing! Then *content*.

Pastor: Thank you for calling me. I remember talking with your parents back then. I'd be happy to catch up with you a bit and see what your need is. Could we get together in my office tomorrow, say at 9 A.M.?

Harry: I guess so. Sure.

Pastor's Silent Reflections: "I guess so." He's probably scared. What does he need from me now on the telephone? Assurance.

Pastor: I'll be happy to meet with you, hear you out, and then see if I have any suggestions to make. I'll do the best I can to be helpful and caring, not critical. Will that be okay?

Harry: Sure. Can't hurt any more than I am now.

Pastor: I'll look forward to meeting you tomorrow morning at 9. Take care. Goodbye.

The next morning the pastor arrived at his office and read his notes on Jim and Mary. When his secretary arrived a few minutes before 9 he told her that he needed not to be interrupted when Harry arrived. At 10 minutes past nine Harry still had not arrived. The pastor nurtured himself by silently affirming: "Harry will be here. He's scared and with good reason. Hard telling how much prejudice he's faced already. Be prepared for him to be suspicious." Moments later Harry came in.

Pastor: Good morning, Harry. Come on in. Have a seat anywhere. Make yourself comfortable. [The pastor does not sit behind his desk and has three very comfortable chairs arranged around a coffee table.]

Harry: Okay.

Pastor's Silent Reflections: Harry seems flat, no energy. He's probably wondering what is going to happen next. From what I know, he unconsciously fears me as a father figure who will treat him just as Jim does. How would his father relate to him now? Start telling him what to do—with some anger and little warmth. I need not to be like his father as I listen.

Pastor: Sometimes people want to come by to talk about something that is troubling them. I listen and care. Sometimes I pray with them; sometimes not. I may have some suggestions for them; maybe not. My intent is never to criticize but to give love just the way I want to be loved when I am hurting. I wonder, then, would you feel okay giving me a thumbnail sketch of what prompted you to call me?

Harry: Well, I understand that my parents told you that I am . . . gay?

Pastor: I'd rather not quote anything they might have said to me. That is part of my commitment to you also. What you share here is private between us.

Commentary: This is a strong rapport-building statement by the pastor. He has now made it clear that he is not a representative of Harry's parents. He is relating to Harry as a person in his own right. Harry's trust of the pastor has probably increased now.

Harry: Well, they told me that they have done some counseling with you and that they felt better afterward. That's why I am here. I think I need some help, but I'm not sure.

Pastor's Silent Reflections: Take your time. Don't rush in with reassurances. Let him do it his way.

Harry: [after a half-minute of somewhat strained silence] Well, I guess I am gay. I've been living with this guy, Al, for about two years. My parents found out about it a year ago. They hate Al, and maybe they hate me. Al moved out Saturday and says we are through. I hate to lose him. I'm feeling very let down. I don't want to go through this again. I don't know what to do.

Pastor's Silent Reflections: Harry is not sure whether I can help him or whether anyone can help him. He may be reluctant to ask me what hope there is for him.

Pastor: Sounds like you've lost a lot of hope these days.

Harry: Yeah! I hadn't quite thought of it that way but you're right. What can I do? I don't believe I can become straight; I don't want to go on being homosexual. I just haven't got it in me to be celibate the rest of my life. I feel stuck!

Pastor's Silent Reflections: He seemed assured that I understood. Now he may be testing me to see if I will tell him his only option is to be straight. I think I need to affirm him more.

Pastor: I like the way you have generated options and have begun checking out possibilities.

Harry: Well, I don't want to go on like this. Something's got to happen.

Pastor: Do you want to consider going straight?

Harry: Now, don't get on my back about that! Damn! I hoped you would be on my side. [looks at his watch, the door]

Pastor's Silent Reflections: I blew that one. Went too fast. Sounded like his father. Dear Lord, please help redeem my relationship with Harry! What is grace like here? Admit my error so that he is not the only person in the room in error!

Pastor: I am in error. I regret that. Thank you for sharing your angry disappointment with me. My intent is to love you as you chart your own course, not to impose my values on you.

Harry: [relaxing just a bit] Well, what are your "values" about homosexuals?

Pastor's Silent Reflections: He's still somewhat hostile. Still, he's asking a question now. I need to own my position sometime. Is this the time? Take it easy!

Pastor: Well, the bottom line for me is that God knows all about you and me and loves us regardless of what we have done. In God's sight, I am just as sinful as you are.

Harry: What's *that* supposed to mean?

Pastor: I am strong in my belief that God loves you and me even though we also sin in everything we do.

Harry: I hope so. I thought the Bible teaches that homosexuality is a sin.

Pastor's Silent Reflections: Now, he seems more to be truly asking for my view and he has connected my view with hope. We are doing better!

Pastor: Yes, the Bible does teach that homosexuality is sinful; it "misses the mark," is less than the ideal that God wants for all of us. The Bible also teaches that gossiping and drunkenness and hate are sinful. Married people sin sexually at times when they use each other just for their own release. The big news of the Bible is not that you and I are sinful but that by the power of God's love we can grow and learn and do better.

Harry: Does the Bible teach that homosexuals can change and become heterosexual?

Pastor's Silent Reflections: **Harry seems open, beginning to become even eager, more hopeful now. Don't go too fast though.**

Pastor: Yes. The Bible teaches that all things are possible with God and even refers to some people who were homosexuals and changed after they became Christians. That's in 1 Corinthians 6:9–11.

Harry: I didn't know that. How in the world can I change that much? It's so deep in me. I knew I was different even as a little boy.

Pastor: I can understand that. If you were inviting me to change my sexual orientation, I would think a lot like you! If you decide to go for change, I will be happy to spend time with you, pray with you, believe in you. In addition, I would want to bring in someone who is more trained and experienced in helping people make such changes. Can we talk about that for a few minutes?

Harry: You mean you want to refer me to a psychiatrist!

Pastor: No. I had in mind a Christian psychologist whom I know here in town. He has worked with homosexual people before and some of them have gained strength to make the change. There is also a Christian support group here for gays going straight.

Harry: I never heard of that! What kind of group?

Pastor's Silent Reflections: **He's getting more excited. He is beginning to believe there is hope. He wants more information about the group. I want to talk more about referral to the psychologist. Go with his agenda, not mine!**

Pastor: It is called Exodus and is somewhat like AA, part of a nationwide network of such groups. My understanding is that people who are in support groups and in private therapy at the same time are much more empowered to reach their growth goals.

Harry: I didn't know you were so involved in all this.

Pastor's Silent Reflections: **This is the first time he has tuned in to me as a person. I want to reinforce that.**

Pastor: Thank you. I am happy to help people with short-term counseling and with referrals to people who can help in other ways.

Harry: Oh, yeah, you mentioned this psychologist. Is he expensive?

Pastor: He charges a professional fee. Most people's health insurance will reimburse for much of the cost of his services. Perhaps your policy will cover that. If you decide to see him, feel free to ask him how he handles fees and insurance.

Harry: Maybe I ought to see him. Couldn't hurt to go once anyway.

Pastor: Good for you. I know that takes courage. His name is Dr. Robert Williams and his office is in the Arcade building near the shopping center two blocks north of here. Here is his phone number. What I'd like to do, with your permission, is to call him and tell him about this talk we've had and tell him that you will be calling him today or tomorrow for a first interview. How would that be?

Harry: Yeah. Okay.

Pastor's Silent Reflections: Now that he is committed, he is feeling more scared. What kind of reassurance would he be most receptive to? I'd like to pray with him but my hunch is he'd dislike that. I could give some man-to-man affirmation. That's a big need of Harry's that probably set him up for homosexual behavior in the first place.

Pastor: Good for you, man! I'm very encouraged that you've got the guts to go meet this guy and see what kind of goals you could reach with him. Way to go! And I'd like to spend some more time like this with you whenever you want to and see if there are ways I can also help. I am committed to giving you all the support I can over the months ahead. How about our setting a time for us to get together two weeks from now just to see what your impressions of Dr. Williams are and what kind of progress you are making?

Harry: [surprised] Yeah! Thank you. I'd like that.

Pastor: Well, this is a Tuesday, the 7th. How about we meet at 9 A.M. on the 21st?

Harry: Sure. I can do that.

Pastor: Great. I'll look to see you then. I'll call Dr. Williams right now to get things moving. In the meantime I just want you to know that I believe that God is with you and will strengthen you and encourage you in whatever lies ahead. Go for it, man! You can make it!

Harry: Thanks, Pastor.

When Harry left, the pastor made some notes for memory jogging when he saw Harry again: 10/7/94 Harry Smith, admitted homosexual whose relationship with Al now broken. Ref. Bob Smith. See Harry on 21st. Harry fears God condemns, doesn't help. He's quick to suspect rejection from me.

The pastor then placed a call to Dr. Williams. Dr. Williams could not come to the phone because he was in therapy. His secretary promised he would soon return the call. The pastor made a note on his "to do" list to expect the call.

This pastor has done a fine, though not perfect, job of taking time to hear Harry out, speaking with Harry in ways that Harry is most receptive, giving support, and making a referral that is likely to be effective. He has planned to continue his care for Harry through later sessions. Harry has already grown a bit in seeing that God's love is freely given, not earned, that he is not a worse sinner than anyone else, and that there is hope for him to build a new life. That is the gospel in action!

Something more is going on here than just Harry facing his homosexuality. He is learning about love and grace and the church and the practical availability of God's power for becoming a new being. Harry has learned that the pastor is willing to suffer with him, to share his own sinfulness, to "come alongside and give support."

References

Paul A. Mickey. 1991. *Of sacred worth*. Nashville: Abingdon Press.

Joseph Nicolosi. 1991. *Reparative therapy of male homosexuality*. New York: Jason Aronson.

Joyce J. and Clifford L. Penner. 1990. *Counseling for sexual disorders*. Dallas: Word Publishing.

11

Caring for God's People

In this final chapter, we want to summarize some of the concepts and statements that underlie this book and its approach to Strategic Pastoral Counseling with sexually troubled people. These concepts and statements, we believe, are biblically based.

First, our sexuality is a gift from God. It is a gift over which God rejoiced (Gen. 1:31): "God saw all that he had made, and it was very good." Furthermore, God placed something of his own image within our humanity (Gen. 1:26). Consequently, the human body and all its functions have God's design, identification, and blessing.

It is not a biblical belief that our body has the bifurcation of body and spirit, the body being base or evil and the spirit more pure and ultimately desirable. Such ideas came from Greek and other pagan philosophies. It was, however, accepted by some Christians in previous periods who believed celibacy a more desirable state and that sexual intercourse was to be only for procreation. Such beliefs are still encountered in the vague feelings of some people that intercourse engaged in for pleasure by married couples has forbidden overtones and cannot be equated with other praiseworthy things in which we celebrate our God-given lives.

The Bible not only declares the human body to have God-given wholeness; it even celebrates sensuality and sexuality. The most notable example is the Song of Songs, which joyfully sings of erotic love.

There are, of course, a number of admonitions in the Bible about sexual thought and conduct but these are focused upon misuse and abuse and not upon sexual expression in its intended purpose and place. It must also be said that even when we do sin through the misuse and misplacement of our sexuality, it is not an unpardonable sin. See how Jesus dealt with the woman at the well (John 4:1–29) and the woman found in adultery (John 8:1–11). In neither case did he condemn; in both cases he sought to redeem and restore. Note also that in John 8:1–11, he dealt first with the men, convicting them of their sin and reminding us that few there are who can throw stones at others.

To help people with their sexual problems we must be approachable. How will people know the pastor is available to talk with them about such intimate or even secret concerns? To some degree, they already know. They have gleaned it from the sermons, pastoral calls, and the ease with which you as pastor have related to them. But if a more conscious effort is to be made to express concern or availability, an occasional sermon could be preached on the stories just mentioned. We can show how Jesus dealt with these persons (and ourselves!) with love and compassion. Note that sexual misconduct was not what he spoke to, for it is often a symptom of a deeper need in life. Instead, he addressed those persons with love, forgiveness, and acceptance, which met that deeper need. You might want to read again the story of David and Bathsheba (2 Sam. 1:1–12, 24). Here we are told of lust, adultery, and murder and yet God accepted David's repentance (Ps. 51) and let David retain his kingship. God also blessed David and Bathsheba with another son, Solomon, the builder of the temple and an ancestor of Jesus.

These and many other such accounts declare the wonderful message of the Bible: God does not want to condemn and destroy but to forgive and restore. Out of his great love for all, he took the burden of our sins, whatever they are, so that we may be free to live and love and enjoy all things that God made for us to be.

With this in mind, let us be understanding and available to those of our people who struggle with their sexuality, remembering that God, who gave us this gift, is with us to help us find fulfillment in our sexuality.

To him who is able to keep you from falling and to present you before his glorious presence without fault and with great joy—to the only God our Savior be glory, majesty, power and authority through Jesus Christ our Lord, before all ages, now and forevermore! Amen. (Jude 24–25)